JACK HILL'S
COUNTRY
FURNITURE

JACK HILL'S
COUNTRY
FURNITURE

WARD LOCK

ACKNOWLEDGEMENTS

I thank all those unknown, early craftsmen whose work has inspired mine and in particular those from more recent times who taught me to love wood, to understand it, and how to make useful things with it.

I acknowledge with gratitude the active participation of Adrian Errey and Tim Boxley who helped in the making of some of the furniture included in the projects. And I thank John Plimmer for his colour photography of the pieces we made. Thanks also to Jenny and Jim Collier and Fran Sansom of Minsted, and to W. L West & Sons who provided locations for the photography. In the making of the book I am most grateful to the publisher and for the contribution and support of Rosie Anderson, Clare Churly, Ruth Baldwin, Caroline Hyams and Gwyn Lewis. And I thank God for the trees we have all used in producing both the furniture and the book.

A Ward Lock Book

Cassell
Wellington House, 125 Strand, London, WC2R OBB

A Cassell Imprint

Text, line drawings and designs copyright © Jack Hill 1998
Photographs © Ward Lock 1998

Distributed in the United States by
Sterling Publishing Co. Inc., 387 Park Avenue South, New York, NY 10016, USA

British Library Cataloguing-in-Publication Data
A catalogue record for this book is available from the British Library

ISBN 0-7063-7606-4

Design by Gwyn Lewis

Photography by John Plimmer

Printed and bound by Kyodo Printing Co., Singapore

All measurements of length in this book are given in inches followed by the metric equivalent in millimetres. Use one or the other: the two systems are not interchangeable.

All the materials, equipment and techniques described in this book are safe if used with care; the author and publishers cannot be held responsible for any injury arising.

Contents

Introduction

O f all the furniture designs and styles which have come down to us over the past centuries, none is today so well liked or so universally esteemed as that which we call country furniture. Pieces made in the village workshops of the seventeenth, eighteenth and nineteenth centuries, for use by a largely rural population more interested in function than in fashion, are now highly regarded and much sought after on account of their sheer simplicity and solid craftsmanship. In our too busy, technological world country furniture has come to epitomize a time and a way of life when the pace is seen to have been much more leisurely; it symbolizes the essence of country living.

But what is country living? What is country furniture? What distinguishes it from other styles of furniture? And is it a style in its own right?

First we must look at the word 'country', which is these days applied to all kinds of seemingly unrelated things, from butter and wine to gardens and household fabrics; is it merely an evocative superlative invented by the advertising men or is it a proper attributive noun? The word comes from the Latin *contra*, meaning 'opposite' or different', and in this context it is the opposite of (sorry, more Latin) *urbanus*, meaning 'of the town or city', from which originates the word 'urban'. Therefore, anything prefixed 'country' – cottage, park, furniture – will be different from similar items which come from or are related to an urban area.

In the past the tag 'country' was often used in a derogatory sense; a country cousin implied someone naive and rather simple. Similarly simple furniture and artefacts of plain construction, made outside the jurisdiction of the largely urban trade guilds and companies, was dismissed as 'country stuff'. But not all urban furniture was necessarily of 'fine' or town quality – not everyone could afford it. Some was made plain and simple, to a price, irrespective of locality.

So, while not all of what we call country furniture was made in the country, it is true to say that most and probably the best of it was. Before 1800 more than three quarters of England's population were rural dwellers and their homes were furnished with simple furniture made locally from local trees.

It is this almost exclusive use of native timbers in the construction of such furniture which provides an important clue in determining its true

origin. While the urban maker would use the more exotic and imported woods fashionable at the time – walnut, mahogany and so on – the rural craftsman would choose local varieties most suited to the work: for resilience in a chair, for example, he would use ash; for strength, oak or elm. His 'exotics' would be the fruitwoods – cherry, apple and pear, or perhaps yew. For more utilitarian purposes he chose beech or pine.

There are two further distinguishing features of country furniture. First, it was most often made to order to fit a specific need. Consequently there is far greater variety in country-made pieces than is found among the 'ready-made' items produced in larger workshops. Second, the maker usually made something he was familiar with, following one of his own – or perhaps his grandfather's – well-tried patterns. As a result little changed; when a piece of furniture proved to be practical, it was repeated over and over again until it became virtually timeless.

Durability was a major consideration of the maker. What was made was made well. It has been rightly said that 'these men did not know how to do a job badly' and long before the present-day mass-manufacturing principle based upon the concept of early repair or replacement, true country furniture was solidly built from well-seasoned material using well-tried methods of construction and mainly hand tools.

It is these same characteristics which contribute to the idea of a country style. A definition of style shows it to refer to a distinctive form of appearance or expression, most often related to a particular period or with regional connotations. As such, style is linked with fashion and subject to change. Country 'style', however, has no such links; spanning more than three centuries, truly universal and uninfluenced by changing fashion, 'country' has outlived other styles and continues to be popular. Because it was simply but sturdily created it possesses that timelessness and an innate naturalness which allow it to blend with other forms of decoration and enhance them. In fact, country style is not really a style at all – it is more a rich heritage of past practices and traditional skills; an expression of good, honest craftsmanship.

The twelve projects in this book are all based on a similar integrity. They represent some of the best of classical country designs and those most popular and useful today. A full description is given on how to make each piece and the making process is explained through the use of concise, step-by-step instructions supported by clear working drawings. To check the accuracy of these instructions each piece of furniture was made either by myself in my own workshop or in association with two colleagues, one an experienced restorer and maker, the other a young man at the beginning of his career. Colour photographs of each finished item are provided for interest and inspiration. The projects vary in difficulty and there is something to suit all levels of ability. For those requiring basic instruction on working practices the book begins with a comprehensive guide to materials, tools and jointing methods.

PART ONE

Materials and Techniques

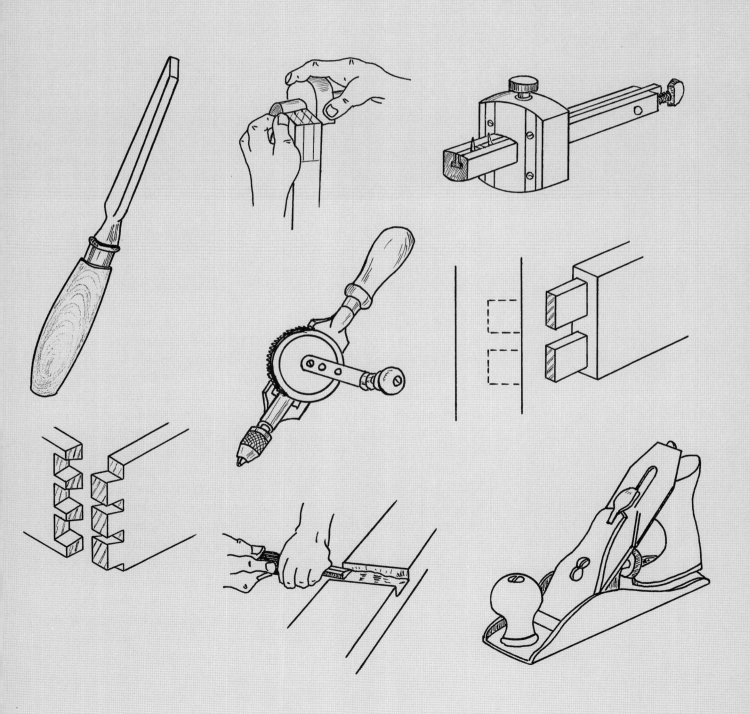

Trees and Wood

The trees which provide us with timber – or wood, or lumber; these terms are synonymous – are divided into two main groups: coniferous (the needle-leaved cone bearers) and deciduous (the broad-leaved species). Additionally, these two groups are known as softwoods and hardwoods respectively, a botanical classification which does not in every case reflect the actual 'softness' or 'hardness', and therefore the working properties, of the wood produced. The softwood yew and some pines are quite hard, for example, while some species of lime and the lightweight balsa wood – both classified as hardwoods – are in fact much softer than many softwoods. And while it is said that hardwoods are more difficult to work than softwoods, this too can be misleading; sycamore and beech, both hardwoods, are easier to work and are said to be 'kinder' than, for instance, a knotty pine or a brittle cedarwood, both of which are softwoods.

Softwood trees, primarily pines, grow mainly in the northern hemisphere across Europe and North America, often in extensive, man-made forest. Relatively fast-growing, they produce tall, straight trunks which, when converted into boards at the saw mill, are suitable for many purposes including joinery and some furniture making. Commercially cultivated and economically harvested, the softwood species in general are less expensive than most hardwoods.

Hardwood trees, of which there are many different species, are widely distributed throughout the world, largely in the temperate and tropical regions. Most, but not all, hardwoods are quite slow-growing, producing denser, more durable timber, well suited to high-class joinery and fine furniture making. Hardwoods provide a wider range of colour, texture and grain figure and are usually more expensive than softwoods.

Before the wood from trees can be used for joinery or furniture making it must be converted – that is, sawn from the round log into boards of usable sizes. For economic reasons most trees are sawn 'through and through', along their entire length, to produce boards of a specified thickness that have sapwood and bark on both edges. An alternative and more desirable method of conversion is known as quarter sawing, though this is rarely done today. However, it is worth noting that two or three of the centre boards from a through-and-through-sawn tree are, in effect, 'quarter' sawn.

OPPOSITE
Jack Hill selects prime English oak at a saw mill in West Sussex

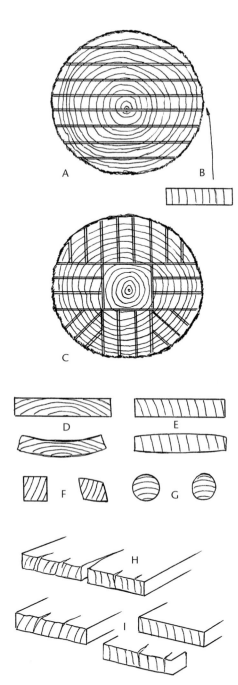

A *Sawn 'through and through'*

B *Quarter sawn centre board*

C *Quarter sawn arrangements*

D *Tangential shrinkage*

E *Radial shrinkage*

F *Square section shrinkage*

G *Round section shrinkage*

H *Heart shake (splitting)*

I *End shake (splitting)*

After conversion wood must be stacked and seasoned (that is, dried) before use. The two methods of drying are by air and kiln. Air drying relies on the action of the sun and on air circulating around the wood outdoors, while the usual method of kiln drying uses a combination of artificial heat and steam in an enclosed space. Air drying – the traditional method – takes much longer than kiln drying; the first is measured in years, the second is reduced to a matter of weeks. The degree of dryness of wood, after seasoning, is quoted as its 'moisture content', or 'MC', and about 12 per cent is recommended for the majority of interior woodworking. If wood which is not properly dry is introduced into the warm, dry environment of the average centrally heated, double-glazed home of today, the resulting movement of the wood will almost certainly lead to problems.

When buying timber it helps everyone if you have a clear understanding of what you want, how much you need and how to order it most economically. Make a cutting list and take it with you: some timber merchants will supply material dimensioned and planed to your specific list. Otherwise, remember to add an allowance for waste: the cutting lists given in the projects which follow are bare sizes and require a waste allowance to be added. Decide on the material to be used, choosing that which is most suitable rather than the cheapest. Look out for defects in the timber, such as splitting, warping, twisting, knots, staining, insect and fungal attack and handling damage.

Timber merchants – or saw mills – and other types of retail outlets usually supply most commercially available softwoods and hardwoods, home-grown and imported. In Britain the timber trade, and in particular many of its customers, have not fully adopted metrication and both metric units (metres and millimetres) and imperial units (feet and inches and fractions thereof) are in use in the measurement and sale of wood and wood products such as plywood. Where wood is sold by volume the cubic foot is still used as the cubic metre is just too large an amount (over 35 cu ft). Sheet material (plywood and so on) may be measured in superficial feet – or square feet – but thickness is given in millimetres. A cubic foot (1728 cu in), incidentally, is equivalent to a sawn board measuring 12 ft in length, 12 in wide and 1 in thick. For small quantities it is usual to quote a price per piece or per foot (or per metre) for a given measured section: for example, 2 × 2 in (or 51 × 51 mm or whatever). In the USA (where the metric system is not used) the standard measurement for wood is the board foot, which is equal to a board 1 in thick and 12 in square.

Wood, particularly softwoods, may be bought either 'sawn' or 'prepared' (that is, planed); sizes quoted are known as 'nominal' (that is, the dimensions before planing). So beware that 'prepared' timber is smaller in cross-section than the nominal size given and that you might have to order the next size up to get what you want. Nominal sizes are fairly standardized throughout the trade. All softwoods are generally sold 'square-edged' (that is, with both long edges sawn parallel). Hardwoods may be bought in three ways: as sawn waney-edge boards (that is, with both edges irregular and the bark still attached) or with one or both edges sawn square. Increasingly it is possibly to buy good-quality hardwoods by 'the piece' and although this is usually a more expensive method of purchasing it is often less wasteful.

The country furniture makers of old would have used wood from locally grown trees and the following lists give brief descriptions of some of the more commonly used woods.

Hardwoods

Tree	Description of wood	Working properties
Ash (Fraxinus excelsior)	White to light brown; coarse texture; distinctive figure.	Tough, resilient, but easy to work and takes a good polish; stable and durable indoors.
Beech (Fagus sylvatica)	Pale yellow to pinkish brown, brown speckle in grain; fine, even texture; little figure.	Hardwearing, clean and easy to work; stains and polishes well; fairly stable.
Cherry (Prunus avium)	Reddish brown; a fine, even-textured, decorative wood with a silky sheen.	Medium hard, tough; works well with sharp tools; finishes well; stable.
Elm (Ulmus procera)	Dull, pale beige to brown; coarse texture, interlocking grain; attractive figure.	Hard and tough, but does not resist sharp tools; stable when well seasoned.
Maple (Acer saccharum)	White to pale yellow; fine texture; has a natural lustre but little figure.	Heavy, hard to very hard; hardwearing and finishes well; reasonably stable.
Oak (Quercus robur)	Cream to medium brown; coarse but even texture; attractive figure with medullary 'rays'.	Strong, hard and durable; works well and takes a good finish; fairly stable.

Softwoods

Tree	Description of wood	Working properties
Cedar (Cedrus libani)	Pale yellow, pinkish; soft, slightly open texture; has an aromatic smell which discourages moths.	Soft, easy to work; straight grain but slightly brittle; polishes to a good finish.
Scots Pine (Pinus silvestris)	Pale, reddish brown; often distinctive figure, especially around knots; may be resinous.	Soft; works easily and well; takes stain and polish or can be painted.
Yellow Pine (Pinus strobus)	Pale yellow to orange-brown; coarse but even texture; may be resinous.	Works fairly easily and clean with sharp tools; takes a good finish; moderately durable.
Yew (Taxus baccata)	Orange to rich brown, creamy sapwood; close texture and distinctive figure.	Tough, elastic, hard; irregular grain; can be difficult to work; finishes beautifully.

Tools and Techniques

The tools used in woodworking are many and various and there are no fixed rules about what constitutes a basic or average tool kit. Much depends upon personal preferences – and prejudices – on what kind of work is to be undertaken and on what is affordable. Buying cheap tools is false economy; always buy good-quality products, even if it means having fewer tools to begin with, and take good care of them.

The tools described here include those used in making the projects which follow. The emphasis is on hand tools, which the country furniture maker would have used in the past, and all the projects could be completed using only these tools. However, some of the more helpful and time-saving power tools popular in many of today's workshops are also included.

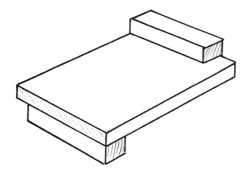

Bench hook

The Workbench The main purpose of this often neglected 'tool' is to provide a working surface and to support the work being done. It should be sturdy enough to withstand the many stresses to which it will be subjected, particularly diagonal movement during planing. The bench should have a reliable means of holding workpieces of various sizes and shapes and this is usually done in a vice of some kind. Other holding devices include 'G' cramps, bench stops and the bench hook. The bench hook is a simple wooden device used primarily to hold work while it is sawn or chiselled. It can be easily home made.

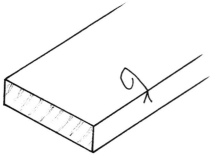

Conventional face side and face edge marks

Measuring and Marking Out All measuring and marking out should be done accurately and checked before cutting – the old adage 'Mark twice and cut once' is well worth remembering. Before beginning any project, make sure that the wood is dry, straight and not warped. Examine the ends of each piece for damage and possible splits: the first inch or so may have to be discarded, so allow waste wood in suspicious areas. Mark and cut ends square before making length measurements; allow waste for saw cuts (kerf) and saw on the waste side of any marked line. Identify the best wide surface and best edge and mark these with the conventional face side and face edge marks. All subsequent marking out is done with reference to these marks.

For general measuring purposes a retractable steel tape is satisfactory,

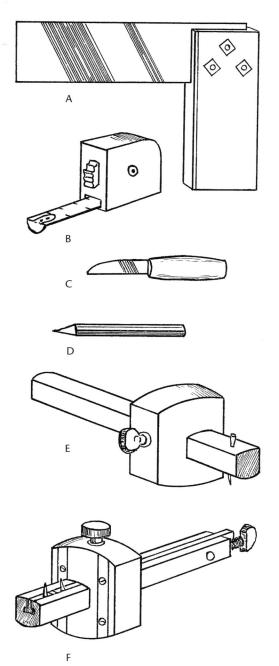

but for more accurate work such as marking out joints and so on a 12-in (305-mm) steel rule is recommended. A well-sharpened HB-grade pencil is suitable for most marking out, but for precise work the point of a sharp knife, used in conjunction with the steel rule, is more accurate and gives an added advantage. The knife cut severs the fibres on the surface of wood which in turn leaves a clean edge after cutting.

For accurate marking across a board, 'square to an edge', you will need a try square, or combination square. For marking lines parallel to a long edge a marking gauge is recommended. Used mainly to mark wood to width and thickness prior to hand planing, it is set by moving and locking the head of the tool the required distance from its pointed spur. Another type of gauge, the mortise gauge, has a double spur and is primarily for use when marking out mortise-and-tenon joints. Combination marking/mortise gauges are available and are a good buy.

Saws and Sawing

Most sawing work at the bench can be done with the tenon saw. This is a type of back saw, its thin blade stiffened by a metal strip, preferably brass. It comes in several sizes with varying numbers of teeth. A 10-in (254-mm) saw with 14 tpi (teeth per inch) is a convenient size for most work. For fine work, such as cutting small dovetails, an 8-in (203-mm), 20-tpi dovetail saw is worth investing in, though a small 'gent's saw' would be a cheaper alternative. A useful but not essential saw, unrestricted by the back strip, is the panel saw; the all-purpose hard-point saw makes a suitable modern substitute for this.

Coarser sawing by hand is carried out with either the rip saw for sawing straight along the grain or the cross-cut for sawing across the grain. With the increased use of power tools and machinery few professionals now use these saws in the workshop and most hobby woodworkers can purchase their material cut close to their requirements. Saws for cutting curved shapes by hand include the coping saw and the fret saw. Both consist of a sprung metal frame and have narrow, disposable blades which, if used carelessly, break easily.

If saws are kept sharp, sawing by hand is not difficult. Many beginners make hard work of it by forcing the saw into the wood and this causes the blade to twist and jam in the saw cut. For easy sawing secure the workpiece properly and begin carefully. If using, say, a tenon saw, pull it backwards on the first few strokes to establish the cut, then work

A *Try square*
B *Steel tape*
C *Marking knife*
D *Pencil*
E *Marking gauge*
F *Mortise gauge*
G *Steel rule*

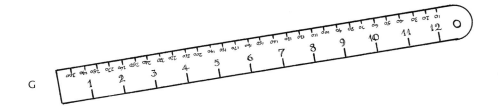

forward with firm but relaxed, fluid strokes, using the full length of the saw blade. When not in use saws should be kept in a suitable rack or hung up to prevent damage to the blade and teeth.

Many sawing operations, particularly initial preparation, can be carried out with hand power tools. Hand-held circular saws can be used for straight cutting, while for both straight and curved cutting there is a choice of the versatile jig saw or small band saw. While the latter is a bench machine rather than a hand-held power tool, it can be a worthwhile addition to the workshop if the amount and type of work justify its purchase.

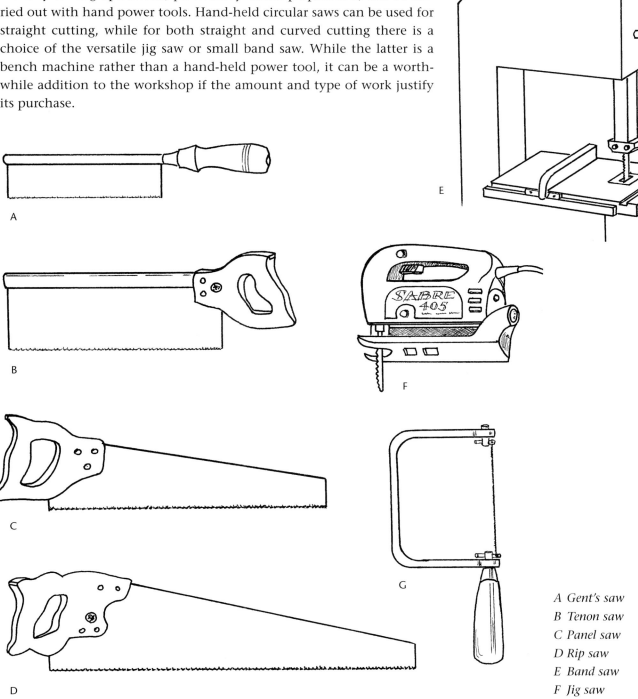

A Gent's saw
B Tenon saw
C Panel saw
D Rip saw
E Band saw
F Jig saw
G Coping saw

***P**lanes and Planing* A metal smoothing plane (Stanley No. 4) is a useful, general-purpose plane, versatile enough to handle most bench work, for bringing wood to size and for surface finishing. The longer jack plane (No. 5) may be substituted – or may be an addition – if much planing is done and especially if long boards are to be planed flat and true. For planing end grain, a sharp smoothing plane, set fine, can be satisfactory, but for best results the lower cutting angle of the small block plane is recommended.

The spokeshave, although not a true plane, cuts in a similar way and is used for smoothing curved edges, cutting chamfers and so on. The old-style wooden ones are nice to use and are occasionally available second-hand. Modern metal spokeshaves are obtainable in either flat or curved sole versions. For an especially fine finish after planing, the cabinet scraper is the ideal tool. Consisting simply of a thin piece of good-quality steel held and flexed between the fingers and thumbs of both hands, its specially sharpened edge can remove shavings as delicate as a butterfly's wing.

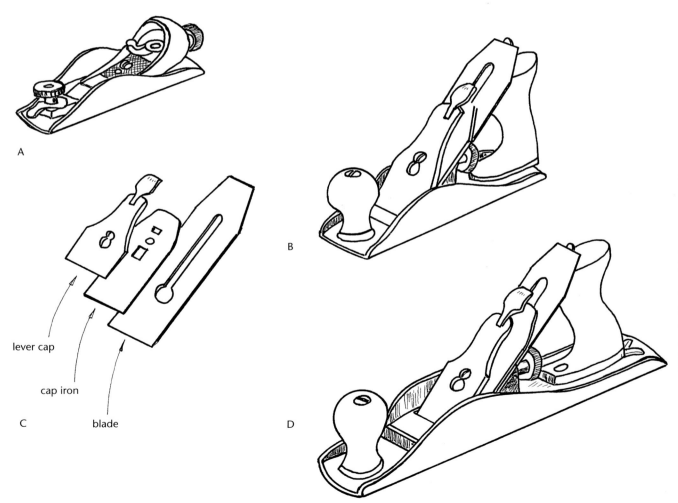

A

lever cap

cap iron

C   blade   D

B

For efficient planing the workpiece must be securely and safely held in place on a stable bench: in the vice for edge planing; between bench stops or with a 'G' cramp for surface planing. To obtain a good finish wood must be planed with the grain and not against it. The plane should normally be set to take the thinnest shaving rather than the thickest and it should be used with long, easy strokes; meanwhile the plane should be kept firm and square to the work and lifted at the end of each stroke. To prevent damage to the cutting edge, planes not in use should not be placed flat on the bench but supported so that the blade is clear of the bench surface or they should be laid on their side.

A variety of hand-held power planers is available. Their rotary cutter block extends across the sole or base of the plane and, while these planes are excellent when planing wood narrower than the width of their sole, they must be used carefully on wood wider than the sole or ridges will occur between adjacent cuts. In this respect it is better to buy 'prepared' or ready planed wood, but remember that it will have been machine planed and will still need some hand planing or scraping to remove the rippled surface left by the rotary cutting action.

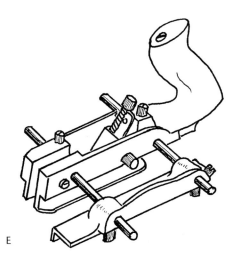

E

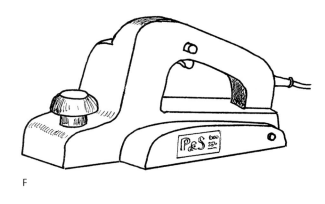

F

G

H

A *Block plane*
B *Smoothing plane*
C *Blade assembly*
D *Jack plane*
E *Plough plane*
F *Electric planer*
G *Wooden spokeshave*
H *Metal spokeshave*

C*hisels and Chiselling*** There is no need to have a complete set of woodworking chisels in their various types and sizes. The most useful are those known as bevel-edged chisels, and to begin with one $3/4$ in (19 mm) and one $1/4$ in (6 mm) wide will suffice; other types and sizes can be added as and when the need arises. The bevel-edged chisel is comfortable to use, its shape allows it to get into tight corners when, say, cutting joints and its handle can be struck lightly with a mallet to give extra force to its cutting action if necessary. If deep mortises are to be chopped out fairly frequently, a $3/8$-in (10-mm) or $1/2$-in (13-mm) mortise chisel should be purchased.

'Chisels' with curved cutting edges, correctly called gouges, are now little used in general woodworking. However, special types of both chisels

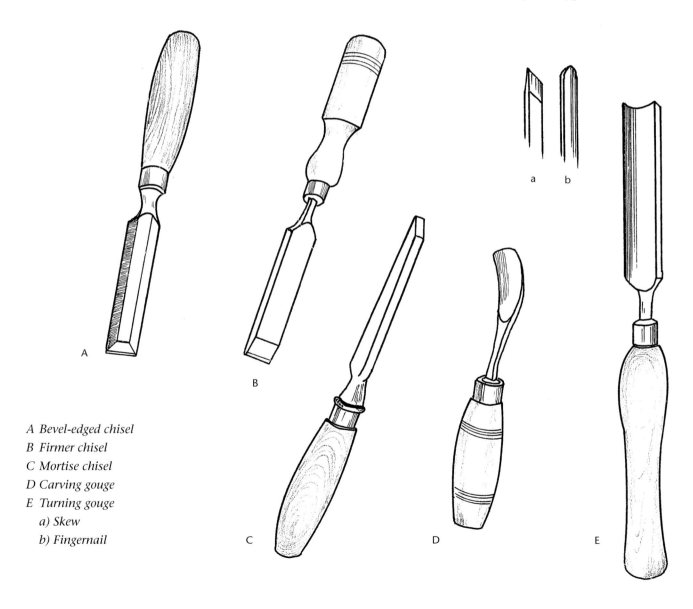

A Bevel-edged chisel
B Firmer chisel
C Mortise chisel
D Carving gouge
E Turning gouge
    a) Skew
    b) Fingernail

and gouges are used in wood carving and in wood turning at the lathe. Wood-carving tools are categorized according to size, shape and sweep (the degree of curvature of their cutting edge) and there are literally hundreds of variations. Selection is a matter of personal choice and requirements. For lathe work chisels and gouges have become highly specialized and their shape and method of grinding and sharpening depends largely upon individual preferences. For the turned work required in the projects, which is all spindle turning, or turning between centres, I use mainly three tools: a heavy, 1^1/$_2$-in (38-mm) roughing-out gouge, a ^{1}/$_2$-in (13-mm) skew chisel and a small, ^{3}/$_8$-in (10-mm) gouge, ground 'finger nail' in shape.

For safety's sake, chisels should be kept sharp at all times – it is easier to have an accident when forcing a blunt chisel into a piece of wood than when guiding a sharp chisel through it. Never hold work with one hand and the chisel in the other: secure the workpiece properly and keep both hands behind the chisel's cutting edge. Make all initial, vertical cuts across the grain and always try to make horizontal cuts with the grain rather than against it.

*S**haping and Smoothing*** Sharp cutting tools produce the best surface finish but there are occasions when other means of shaping and smoothing will be needed. Various kinds of abrading tools may be used for these purposes, the most common being files and rasps or their more modern counterparts. Some of the latter incorporate a disposable blade of thin, hardened steel perforated with multiple sharp-edged holes while others have tungsten-carbide grit heat bonded to both rigid and flexible substrates. These tools, generally speaking, leave an unaccept-able roughened surface which requires further smoothing.

Abrasive sheets can be included here although these are, strictly speak-ing, for finishing and not for shaping. Abrasives are made from one of several natural or artificial materials in small particle form bonded to either paper or cloth backings and are graded according to a number system which describes the particle or grit size – the higher the number, the smaller the grit and, as a consequence, the smoother the abrasive action. The red-coloured garnet paper in grades 100, 150 and 220 will cover most needs. Always use abrasives with the grain of the wood, not across it. And to keep flat surfaces flat, use the abrasive wrapped around a suitable cork sanding block.

For the majority of wood-smoothing operations a wide range of power tools is now available, including belt, drum and disc sanders, and orbital sanders. These devices can save a great deal of time, but some do not always leave a satisfactory finish and should be used with caution. In addition they can produce a lot of environmentally unfriendly noise and dust. Ideally such tools should have their own dust extraction and the operator should wear a dust mask or respirator.

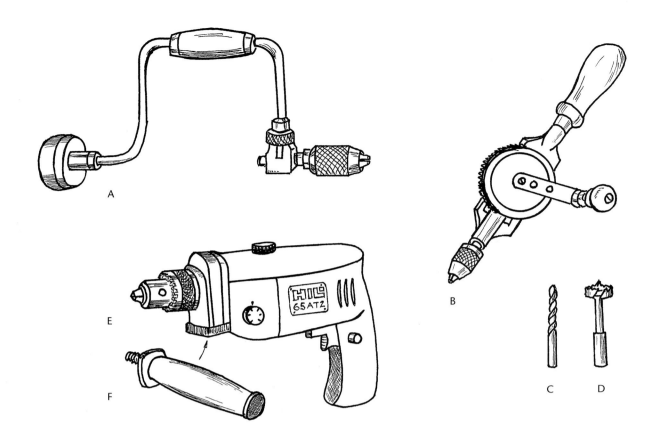

A Ratchet brace
B Wheel brace
C Twist drill
D Forstner bit
E Electric power drill
F Optional front handle

Drills and Drilling The brace and bit was always the traditional tool for boring holes in wood; later, a different form of what is still a hand drill, the wheel brace, came into vogue. Both these tools are still, in use but the relatively low cost of the electric power drill has made it by far the most popular and most commonly used tool for drilling holes in wood (and metal) today. Single-, dual- and variable-speed versions are available and there are both mains electric and battery-powered types to choose from. A vertical stand – there are several models – can be used to convert most hand-held power drills into a simple but effective bench drilling machine. If a large amount of repetitive drilling is undertaken, a purpose-made bench or pillar drilling machine will make life easier and give greater accuracy, so is a worthwhile investment.

Whatever type is used, there is a wide range of drill bits available. For general work up to about 1/2 in (13 mm) diameter, ordinary twist bits (engineer's drills) are suitable for both wood and metal. For more accurate drilling in wood – for dowel jointing, for example – the modified twist bit known as the spur bit is useful. For even greater accuracy, and especially for large holes or holes with flat bottoms, saw-toothed Forstner bits are recommended, but good ones are expensive. If a brace is used, the old type of centre bit is good and so are the ordinary twist bits which can also be used in many of them. For countersinking after drilling (for countersunk screw heads) use a rose head countersink.

C***ramps and Cramping*** Cramps are useful for holding work temporarily and for applying pressure when gluing up. The most common type is the 'G' cramp (or clamp) of which there are several sizes (the maximum opening of the jaws) to choose from. The 6-inch (152-mm) version is a handy size to have. (An alternative to the 'G' cramp is the 'F' cramp, also available in several sizes.) For large-scale work the sash cramp, or bar cramp, is the most useful. There are a number of variations on these two basic forms of cramp, some better than others. A versatile type of cramping device for carcass and frame construction is the webbing cramp.

When using cramps, always protect the surface of the work from damage with blocks of soft wood or other material. When using cramps in a gluing-up operation, have everything ready before beginning – bench clear, cramps set close to the required size and so on – and work quickly. Be sure to protect wood from steel cramps in the vicinity of glue to avoid iron staining.

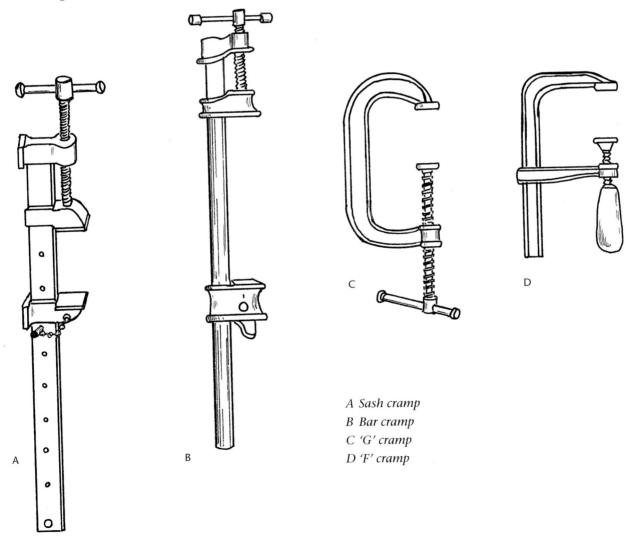

A Sash cramp
B Bar cramp
C 'G' cramp
D 'F' cramp

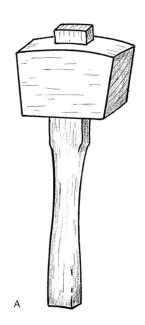
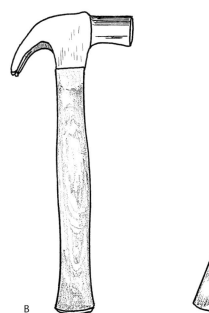
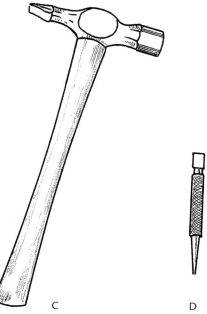

A

B

C

D

A Joiner's mallet
B Claw hammer
C Cross-pein hammer
D Nail set
E Pincers
F Bradawl
G Screw driver (plastic handle)
H Cabinet screw driver (wooden
  handle)

***M**iscellaneous Tools* Miscellaneous tools include a medium-size wood or composition mallet, mainly for use in some chiselling operations and certain assembly processes, and a medium-weight, cross-pein hammer – one about 10 oz (or the metric equivalent) in weight is fine. You will also need a claw hammer or a pair of pincers for the removal of the inevitable bent nail or panel pin, plus a nail set, or pin punch, with which to set them below the surface when they go in correctly. To fit the different sizes of screw commonly used – that is, nos 4, 6 and 8 – two or maybe three different sizes of screw driver will be required; slot-headed screws are more in keeping with country pieces then the cross-head type. For starting screws in softwood, a bradawl is useful; when screwing, or nailing, into hardwood it is best to drill adequate pilot holes.

***S**harpening Equipment* Sharp tools are a prerequisite to producing good work. A cutting edge which is dull not only makes the work difficult but also constitutes a safety hazard. A blunt plane will simply not plane properly and forcing a dull chisel into any piece of wood is a recipe for disaster.

The process of sharpening embraces both grinding and honing, the first done usually on a revolving grindstone which produces a bevel but an edge normally too coarse to be suitable as a cutting edge. After grinding, therefore, the ground edges of tools such as planes and chisels require honing (or whetting) on a sharpening stone of some description. This may be a traditional oil stone, a Japanese water stone or one of the several proprietary 'stones' consisting of diamond dust impregnated in a plastic or ceramic substrate. All types are graded by a grit number, as for abrasives, or by description – fine, medium and coarse. A fine and

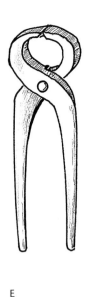

E

F

G

H

medium combination stone is a useful choice to being with. Oil stones are used with a film of light oil on their surface, mainly to float off metal residue produced by the sharpening process and to reduce friction; water is applied to water stones for the same purpose.

New cutting edge tools are usually supplied ground but not honed and require some attention before use; tools which have become dull through use need similar attention. The blade is held at an angle of about 30 degrees to the surface of the stone and rubbed forward and back along the full length of the stone. When a burr has formed at the cutting edge, turn the blade over and, keeping it absolutely flat on the stone, rub off the burr to produce a good cutting edge. Beginners who find it difficult to maintain a constant angle should try keeping the wrists stiff or use a honing guide.

*A**dhesives* The final assembly of a piece of furniture is described as 'gluing up'. It involves using one of several adhesive materials, or glue, now available. Traditionally animal glue was used – it was all there was – and this was heated in a double pot and applied hot. Animal glue is still obtainable; its main attribute is that it can be re-softened by applying moisture and heat – useful in furniture restoration – but it is not notably a strong glue. Today the most convenient and inexpensive adhesives are those based on polyvinyl acetate emulsion (PVA). The majority of these are white or cream, water-soluble liquids supplied ready to use. Excellent general-purpose adhesives, PVA glues are available for use indoors and outside. Where a high level of water resistance is required, urea formaldehyde adhesives are recommended; these have two parts which require mixing before use.

Joints and Working Methods

The purpose of the several different joints used in woodworking is to hold or lock the separate pieces of a construction together in a strong and (usually) permanent way. Factors such as loading stresses, wear and tear and the natural movement of wood have all been taken into account in the design and recommended use of specified joints; each one has been tried and tested over many years and has proved to be best suited to its particular application.

Most jointing methods are based on shaped components interlocking with each other in some way to form, when glued, permanent, rigid fixtures. Other ways of joining wood together make use of metal fastenings such as nails or screws, or use wooden dowels, while some depend solely on the adhesion of glued surfaces or on a combination of these methods. In earlier times joints relied more on wedges or pegs for security than on glue or screws.

Where two or more pieces of wood are to be joined edge to edge to make a wider piece, the tongue-and-groove joint may be used or the edges simply but adequately glued together. When two pieces cross or meet in an 'L' or a 'T' formation, the halving or lap joint or perhaps the bridle joint is used, and when a pair of upright pieces are to support a horizontal piece, as in a shelf, various kinds of housing or dado joint are employed. To join two pieces of wood which meet at a corner, as in a box or drawer, for example, a simple rebate or housing, glued or pinned, can be used. But a much stronger joint is obtained by using one of several types of dovetail joint – particularly for a drawer where tension is put on the joint when the drawer is pulled out. For all kinds of framing purposes dowel joints can be used, but the mortise-and-tenon, in one of its several forms, remains the strongest and most commonly used joint in this instance.

How to make the joints used in the projects which follow, together with some of their variations, is described here. In keeping with the nature of the book, the emphasis is on traditional methods consistent with solid wood construction.

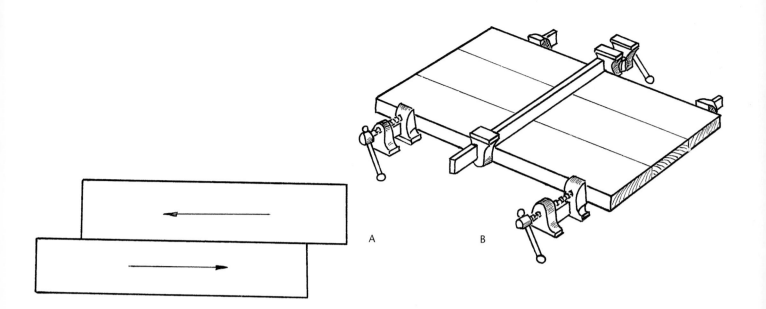

Edge jointing
A Rubbing the joint
B Cramping arrangement

*E*dge Jointing   When it is necessary to join narrow pieces edge to edge to make wide boards or panels, the simple plain edge butt joint is normally used. Traditionally relying on the natural 'tack' of hot animal glue, this was known as the rubbed joint, and while it may be a simple joint it is not necessarily the easiest to make as it calls for accurate planing of the mating edges.

First select the boards to be joined, matching them for colour and figure and reversing the heart of the side of alternate pieces where possible. Mark adjacent pieces. To plane a true edge use the longest plane you have, and to help avoid the common mistake of removing too much at each end try to plane more off in the middle. Using modern adhesives together with cramps, it is better to be slightly hollow there than to be low at the ends. Edges must be square; test by placing boards edge to edge: they should not rock on each other, nor should light be visible between them.

When all edges are true, set up a pair of sash cramps on a level surface open to a little over the required width and have a third cramp nearby. Paper strips should be used to isolate glue from the steel bars to avoid staining. Put glue on one of the adjoining edges and rub the edges together lengthways; this removes surplus glue and rubs glue into the wood fibres. Add further pieces as required, arranged on the two cramps, then place the third cramp on top as shown. Lightly tighten the centre cramp first, then the other two; check that all joints are aligned and test for flatness – the arrangement of the cramps helps in this respect. For long boards use more cramps but in a similar configuration. Wipe off surplus glue and leave to dry; finally clean up with a plane or scraper.

For larger surfaces such as table tops the edges may be shaped – tongued and grooved, for example – to increase the gluing area, or reinforced with dowels, biscuits or loose plywood tongues.

E*nd or Butt Joints*** Since end grain does not provide a good surface for gluing, various methods of jointing two pieces which meet at a corner, as in a box, have been devised. The dovetail (see page 38) is the best answer, of course, but end or butt joints do offer a simple alternative suitable for some applications. The plain butt joint must be glued and can be reinforced with panel pins, but the mitred joint, although more difficult to make, is neater and stronger on account of its increased gluing area. It can be strengthened by wooden splines or keys set in saw cuts made across the corner after gluing.

An improvement on these basic butt joints is to shape the end of one or both mating pieces. This both strengthens the joint by increasing the gluing area and improves its appearance by concealing the end grain. The lap or rebated joint is the simplest and easiest to do. Each piece is cut to length and the square end of the 'side' piece is set into a rebate cut in the end of the 'front' piece. The lap remaining after the rebate is cut covers the end grain of the side piece. The joint is secured with glue and pins driven through the side piece. The alternative housed and groove-and-rebate joint is stronger and does not require pinning.

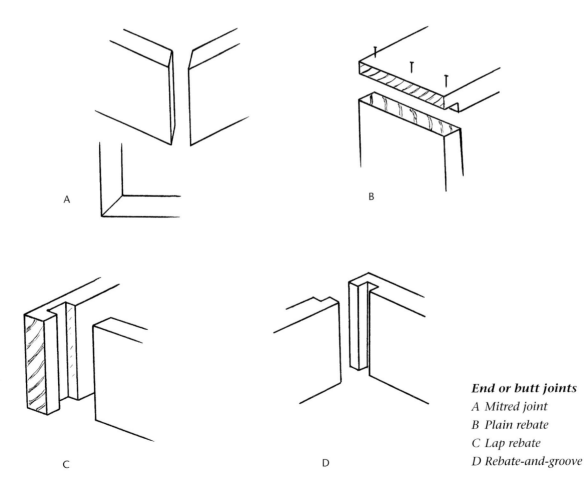

A

B

C

D

End or butt joints
A Mitred joint
B Plain rebate
C Lap rebate
D Rebate-and-groove

Halving Joints For jointing two pieces that meet or cross over each other with their surfaces remaining flush, the halving or lap joint provides a simple solution. It is used mainly in frame construction. There are several variations of this joint and, although they lack the strength of, say, the mortise-and-tenon, they are easy to make and satisfactory in some applications. This type of joint takes its name from the way in which half the thickness of each piece to be jointed is normally cut away to provide a flush-fitting recess. All halving joints are glued and in certain applications some are additionally secured by nails or screws.

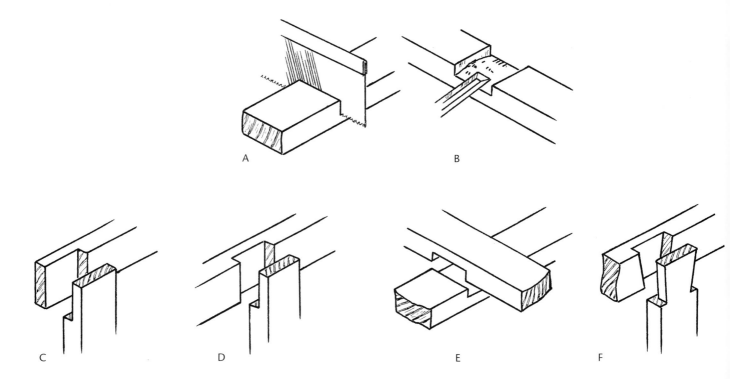

Halving joints

A Sawing vertically

B Chiselling out the waste

C Corner halving joint

D 'T' halving joint

E Cross halving joint

F Dovetail 'T' halving joint

Cross-halving, corner and 'T' joints are the three most common types of this joint and the marking-out procedure is the same in each case. First mark the relative position of each piece, then score straight across with a sharp knife and continue these marks half-way down each side. A marking gauge is then set to half the thickness of the wood and a line gauged between the knife marks. Saw vertically down to the gauged lines on the waste side and chisel out the waste wood. Work equally from both sides to finish flat across the full width. Careful paring with a sharp chisel will produce a neat, tight-fitting joint.

A useful alternative to the normal 'T' joint is the dovetail 'T' halving joint. Begin by marking out and cutting the dovetail and use this as a template to mark the recess for it. A stopped version of this joint is used when the end of the joint is to be concealed.

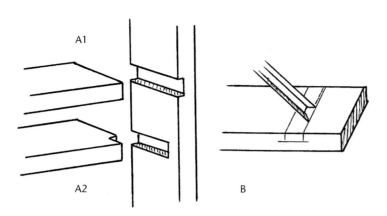

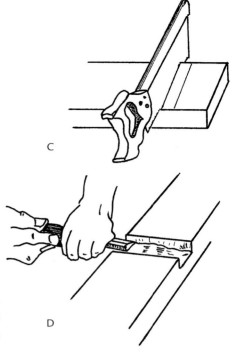

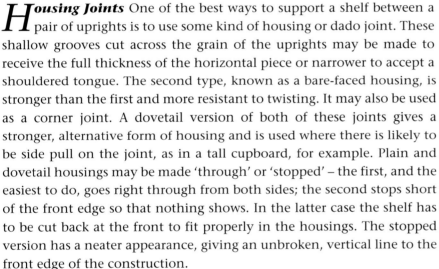

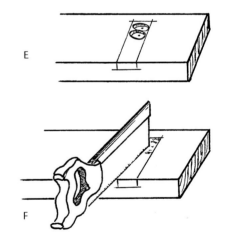

Housing Joints One of the best ways to support a shelf between a pair of uprights is to use some kind of housing or dado joint. These shallow grooves cut across the grain of the uprights may be made to receive the full thickness of the horizontal piece or narrower to accept a shouldered tongue. The second type, known as a bare-faced housing, is stronger than the first and more resistant to twisting. It may also be used as a corner joint. A dovetail version of both of these joints gives a stronger, alternative form of housing and is used where there is likely to be side pull on the joint, as in a tall cupboard, for example. Plain and dovetail housings may be made 'through' or 'stopped' – the first, and the easiest to do, goes right through from both sides; the second stops short of the front edge so that nothing shows. In the latter case the shelf has to be cut back at the front to fit properly in the housings. The stopped version has a neater appearance, giving an unbroken, vertical line to the front edge of the construction.

In making housing joints, it is best to mark the shelf thickness from the actual shelf to avoid inaccuracies. To make the plain through housing, first square a pencil line across the inside face of the upright to mark the top edge of the groove, then position the end of the shelf on this line and mark both sides with a sharp knife pressed close against the shelf. Continue these marks about 1/4 in (6 mm), or no more than one third the thickness of the upright, down each side. Set a marking gauge to a similar measurement and mark the depth of the housing. Mark the uprights in pairs to ensure that the shelf ends are of equal height and level. Deepen the knife cuts and chisel a sloping cut into the waste side of each to act as a guide for the saw, then saw carefully down to the depth line. Remove the waste wood by chiselling, working inwards from both edges. Finish by careful levelling.

For the stopped joint, mark out as described above, but mark the depth of the groove on the back edge only. Mark in from the front edge,

Housing joints
A1 Through housing
A2 Stopped housing
B Sloping cut helps guide saw
C Sawing down to depth line
D Chiselling out waste
E Holes drilled to clear end of stopped joint
F Sawing the stopped housing

about 1/2 in (13 mm) and cut a recess, or drill two or three overlapping holes of the required depth, within the marked lines – this clears a space for the point of the saw. Saw carefully and chisel out as before. On the shelf mark the cut-out for the front edge and saw the shoulder back fractionally short so that it pulls up tight against the upright piece when assembled. Both these types of housing can be cut more quickly if you take out the bulk of the waste by drilling a series of holes between the sawn lines; use a flat-bottomed Forstner bit. Alternatively, housing grooves can be cut with a portable electric router.

The dovetail housing is more difficult to do by hand, the one-sided (bare-faced) version being the easier of the two types. For this, the shelf is marked out and cut first. With a marking gauge set at one third the thickness of the upright, mark a shoulder line on the underside of the shelf and continue it over on to the edges. Mark an adequate slope for the 'tail'. Knife out the shoulder line, chisel a sloping cut into it to guide the saw and saw carefully down to the marked 'tail' line. Chisel away the waste wood – a shaped guide block may be found helpful in maintaining the angle both for sawing and chiselling. The stopped version follows the same procedure as described above. For the full, double-sided dovetail housing both sides of the shelf are marked out and cut as described and the housing itself is cut at an angle on both sides. To be effective the dovetail must be tight yet free enough to slide into the housing from one end. Although it is difficult to make by hand, it can be relatively easy if you use a portable electric router fitted with a dovetail cutter.

***M**ortise-and-tenon Joints* In one or other of its many variations the mortise-and-tenon joint is the most commonly used type for framing and carcass construction where maximum strength is required. The basic form of the joint is the through mortise and tenon consisting of a recess or hole (the mortise) cut into and, in this case, through one piece of wood (the stile) and a reduced, shouldered projection (the tenon) on the end of the joining piece (the rail) which fits into it. Tightly held, glued, and sometimes wedged or pegged, this makes a very secure and mechanically strong joint. Its alternative forms described here are made for additional strength, for special circumstances or for aesthetic reasons.

All mortises and tenons follow the general principle that where joining pieces are of equal thickness the tenon should be approximately one third the thickness of the pieces – it is usually more precisely decided by the width of chisel available. Where a stile is more substantial, the tenon can be thicker. Where a mortise is close to the end of a stile and in doors, for example, it is usual to have some extra length at each end to reduce the risk of splitting while cutting the joint. These waste pieces, known as horns, are sawn off later.

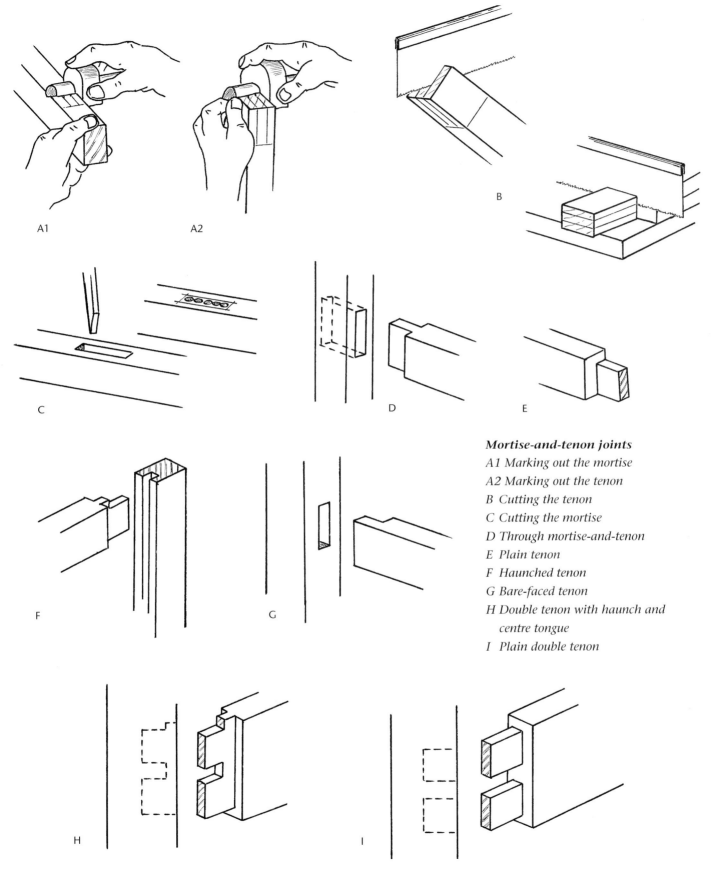

Mortise-and-tenon joints

A1 Marking out the mortise
A2 Marking out the tenon
B Cutting the tenon
C Cutting the mortise
D Through mortise-and-tenon
E Plain tenon
F Haunched tenon
G Bare-faced tenon
H Double tenon with haunch and
   centre tongue
I Plain double tenon

Testing the fit and accuracy of a newly cut tenon into its accommodating mortise

The joint used in several of the projects which follow is the stub or stopped mortise-and-tenon; in this joint the mortise is 'blind' – that is, not cut through – and the tenon is correspondingly shortened so that end grain does not show on the opposite surface. Two types are described: plain and haunched.

To make this joint, first mark the position and width of the mortise on the edge of the stile. This can be the full width of the rail, or the tenon can be edge shouldered, plain or haunched. For corner joints – as in door frames and carcasses – the tenon must be edge shouldered and the mortise made to suit. Measure and cut the rail to length – shoulder length plus the length of two tenons – and mark the shoulder length lines all round with a sharp knife. Set the twin spurs of a mortise gauge to the required one third or thereabouts and, working from the face side, mark the width of the mortise and the thickness of the tenon across the end of the rail and down each side to the shoulder line at the same setting.

Cut the mortise first; remove the waste by chiselling or by drilling followed by chiselling. Avoid levering the chisel against the edge of the mortise as this will compress the wood and spoil the edge. The mortise depth should be a little more than the tenon length. Now cut the tenon; first, with the rail held upright in a vice, use a tenon saw to cut down the waste side of each gauged line as shown on page 33, reverse and finish carefully down to the shoulder line. Then, with the rail held flat, saw down at the shoulder line to remove the waste wood from each side. Cutting a guide groove for the saw, as described under housing joints (page 31), helps achieve neat-fitting shoulders. Ideally tenons should fit mortises straight from the saw, but some trimming with a chisel may be necessary.

A certain amount of reduction in tenon width is usual in most joints and essential in some. A small edge shoulder will conceal any damage at the end of the mortise, while for corner joints a more substantial reduction (usually equal to one quarter the width of the tenon) is necessary. To prevent any twisting of the rail a small portion of the tenon is retained. This haunch, as it is called, is also employed in the mortise and tenon used at the corners of panelled doors, where it not only helps strengthen the joint but also fits and fills the exposed end of the panel groove in the stile. Conveniently the joint should be made the same width as the groove and is normally cut after the groove is made.

The double mortise-and-tenon is used when jointing wide rails to stiles. In such situations a simple long mortise would weaken the stile, while a wide tenon might become loose through shrinkage. The joint is marked out as shown on page 33; the mortise, including the centre recess, is cut first and the double tenon and tongue cut and trimmed to fit.

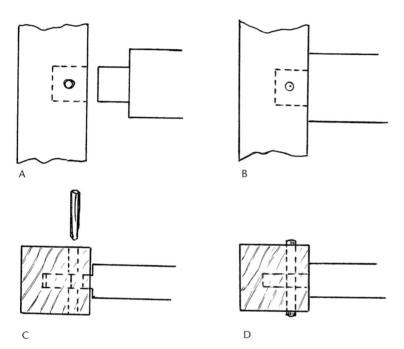

A

B

C

D

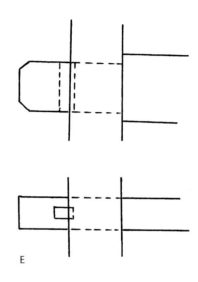

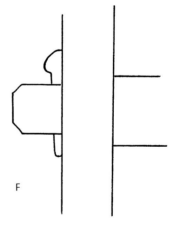

Special mortise-and-tenon joints
A, B, C, D Draw boring: pegged joint
E, F Loose key tenon joint

E

F

A traditional method of tightening up and securing a mortise-and-tenon joint is by pinning or pegging it. This is often incorrectly done in modern reproduction furniture by simply drilling into the assembled joint and fitting a dowel. Correctly known as draw boring, this should be done by drilling the hole through the stile before the tenon is inserted. The tenon is then pushed in to full depth and the same size drill used just to mark the surface of the tenon. The tenon is removed and re-marked about 1/16 in (1 mm) in towards the joint shoulder and drilled at this point. The slight offset will draw the joint tight when the peg is driven in. Pegs are usually hand cut and tapered to ease starting. Protrusions are cut off on completion.

A traditional type of mortise-and-tenon, which provides in effect a 'knock-down' facility, is the loose key tenon. This joint, based on the old carpenter's tusk tenon, has a long, shouldered tenon which passes through a mortise in the stile where it is secured by a wedge (the key) driven through a slot cut through the tenon. This slot must be positioned just into the mortise so that the wedge bears and tightens against the stile. This fixing allows the joint to be demountable and is used particularly on the stretcher rails of trestle tables, benches and so on.

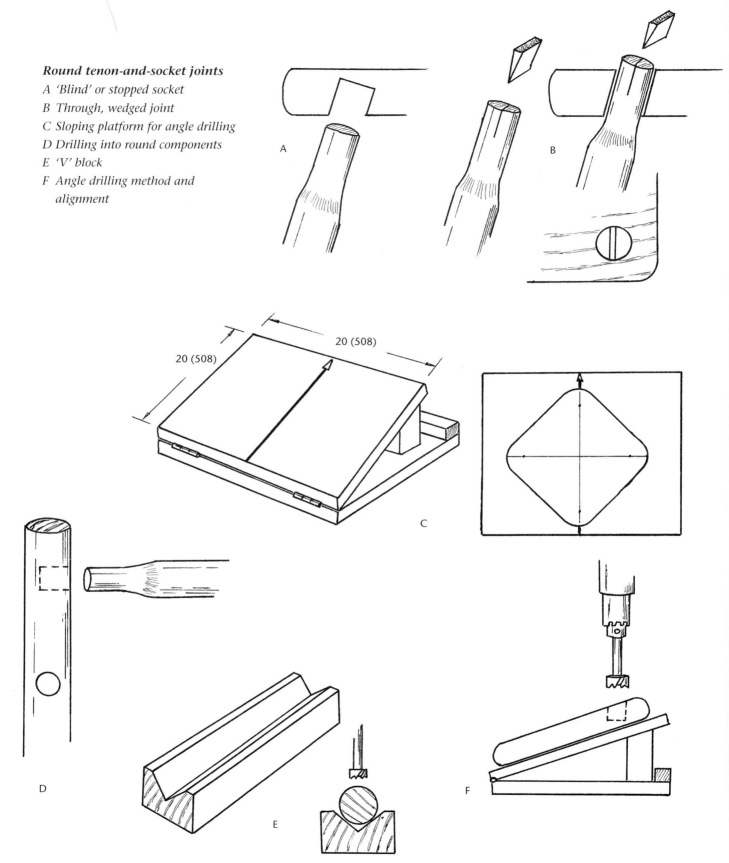

Round tenon-and-socket joints

A 'Blind' or stopped socket
B Through, wedged joint
C Sloping platform for angle drilling
D Drilling into round components
E 'V' block
F Angle drilling method and
   alignment

20 (508)

20 (508)

A

B

C

D

E

F

Round Tenons and Sockets   It is common and expedient, in some types of stool and chair construction, particularly those of the 'country' variety, to join round components together by means of round tenons fitted into round sockets. Sockets are accurately and easily drilled to match the diameter of the (usually) turned components which should be a friction fit. Sockets may be 'through' or 'blind' (stopped). Through joints are normally wedged for added security and where this is done wedges must lie at right angles to (in other words, across) the grain of the seat surface, otherwise the wood will be split when the wedge is driven in.

Some woodworkers advocate tapered tenons and sockets, but straight, parallel-sided holes and well-fitting parallel tenons give a better joint – and are easier to make. Sockets are best drilled with a saw-toothed Forstner bit (see page 22) and tenons may be reduced to size by being turned on a lathe or rounded using any appropriate tool; if necessary, they may be whittled with a knife or chisel and finished with abrasives. A general rule of proportion is that the socket depth (if drilled blind) should be at least equal to the tenon diameter.

These joints are frequently required to be made at angles other than 90 degrees. This means drilling sockets consistently at a given angle, which is not easy to do by hand and eye alone. To overcome the problem the use of suitable jigs in conjunction with a bench or pillar drill, which provides an accurate vertical reference, is recommended. The adjustable sloping platform jig shown on page 36 may be set to any required simple angle while orientation about the centre line on the jig helps when drilling compound angles. The 'sight lines' marked on work to be drilled, as shown, are aligned with this centre line for repeated accuracy. For drilling into round components a simple 'V' block as shown will hold work firm and ensure accuracy.

Dowel Joints   Regarded by some as an inferior substitute for the mortise-and-tenon joint, dowelled joints, using the modern fluted dowels in deep, well-fitting holes, can be as strong and are considerably easier to make. Dowelled joints have numerous applications, particularly in carcass and frame construction and in strengthening edge to edge joints (see page 28).

Mating pieces should be true and square and the drilled holes perfectly aligned. Dowel positions may be marked out by measurement or with the aid of a simple template. Various proprietary jigs are also available and these can increase accuracy and reduce the amount of marking out required. A simple way is to mark out one piece by measurement, knock panel pins into the dowel centre marks and cut off their heads to leave about 1/8 in (3 mm) protruding. Then hold the mating piece in the correct position and press it down on the pins. Remove the remains of the pins and drill exactly on their marks and their opposite impressions.

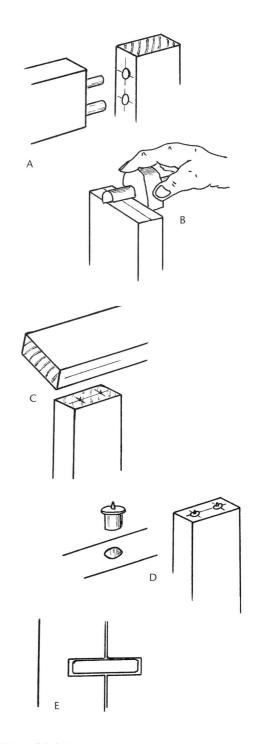

Dowel joints

A Typical dowelled joint

B Marking out

C Positioning with panel pins

D Positioning with dowel markers

E Drilled sockets should be deeper than half the dowel length

JOINTS AND WORKING METHODS   **3 7**

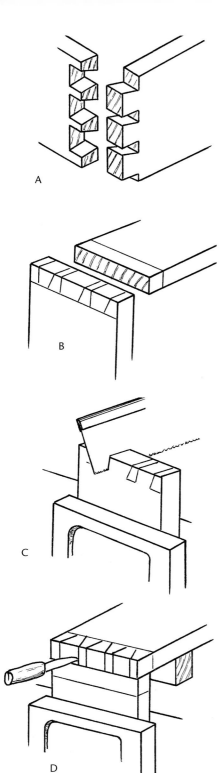

A similar method uses proprietary dowel markers; holes are marked and drilled into one piece, appropriate sized markers are inserted and the mating piece pressed on to them to impress the opposite centres.

Drilled holes should always be a little deeper than half the length of the dowel to allow full entry and accommodate surplus glue; counter-sinking prevents rough edges interfering with the close fitting of the joint surfaces. Plain dowels, if used, require a saw cut along their length to allow compressed air and glue to escape and they benefit from being chamfered at either end to aid entry. The modern fluted dowels eliminate the need for these precautions and in addition the fluting process compresses the wood fibres which swell when glue is applied, thus tightening their fit.

*D*ovetail Joints The dovetail is the strongest corner joint for box and drawer construction. Its strength lies in the increased gluing area and the mechanical advantage in the shape of the interlocking parts. There are several variations, the two most common being the through (or common) dovetail and the lapped dovetail. In through dovetails end grain tails and pins show on both sides of the joint, while in the lapped version end grain tails are concealed on one face. The latter joint is the one usually chosen for drawer fronts.

It is usual to mark out and saw the tails on one piece first and then use that as a pattern to mark out pins and sockets on the mating piece and cut these last. Before cutting ensure that the ends of pieces to be jointed are true and square and to the required length plus about 1/16 in (1 mm) for cleaning-up purposes.

In box construction, where the pieces are of equal thickness and the through dovetail is used, begin by setting a sharp marking or cutting gauge to the thickness of the wood and mark lightly all round both ends of each piece. This is the depth line of the joint. Mark out the position of the separate tails on the end of the 'tail piece', then mark in the angle or rake of the tails using a sharp pencil and either a sliding bevel or a dovetail template. Saw carefully on the marked lines down to the depth line. To mark out the pins, place the 'pins piece' upright in a vice and support the tail piece so it lies on it true and square to its front edge. Using a sharp knife, or the point of the saw, mark through the saw cuts of the tail piece and square these lines down to the depth line. To avoid mistakes clearly mark the waste area, then saw the pins on the waste side of the marked line. Remove the bulk of the waste from both pieces with a coping saw and clean up with a sharp chisel, working from both sides. Do not go beyond the depth lines.

For drawer work, where forward concealment of the joint is required, the lapped dovetail is used. For this it will be found convenient to have the front piece about one quarter to one third thicker than the side pieces and to make tail lengths equal to the side piece thickness. Set a marking or cutting gauge to the tail length thickness and mark lightly all

Dovetail joints

A Through dovetail
B First stage in marking out
C Sawing the tails
D Marking the pins and sockets

round the end of the side piece, or 'tail piece'. Gauge mark the end of the front piece (pin or socket piece) from the inside surface, as shown. Mark out the tails and their rake on the end of the tail piece, as in the through dovetail, and saw these down to the depth line. Place the front piece upright in a vice and support the side piece on it, true and square to the gauged 'lap' line. Mark through as described above and mark out the waste area.

Remove the waste wood from the tail piece as described. To remove the waste from between the pins on the front piece, keep it upright in the vice and saw carefully at an angle on the waste side of the marked line to the lap and depth line. Part of the waste can be sawn away, but most must be removed by careful chiselling. Do this with the wood held to a flat board clamped to the bench and begin with vertical cuts across the grain, then with the grain, to ease out the waste, working back to the gauged lines. Use a narrow bevel-edged chisel and make sure that the inside corners are properly cleaned out. An alternative way of removing the bulk of the waste is to bore it away using a Forstner bit (see page 22).

Dovetail joints, and others, can also be made using special jigs in conjunction with a portable electric router. Variations of the dovetail joint include secret double lap and mitred dovetails and those used in carcass or frame construction, mainly single or double dovetails and those similar to the dovetail 'T' halving joint (see page 30).

*F*inishing Methods   While the materials and the standard of craftsmanship determine the quality of a piece of work, its final appearance will depend upon the surface finish which is applied. Most finishes are used to protect the surface by sealing the pores of the wood and this in turn helps to minimize the adverse effects of sunlight, movement due to shrinkage, and other problems caused by environmental conditions. Some finishes, such as opaque paint, are used to obliterate or disguise the surface, while transparent finishes such as clear varnishes and polish, oils and waxes serve to enhance and emphasize the natural features of the wood. Additionally, most finishes give some resistance to everyday use and many can be renewed as time and possible abuse require.

Before applying any surface finish, ensure that the wood is absolutely clean and smooth. Residual grease, dirt or dried glue will repel the finishing material, while scratches and any rough areas will be accentuated – especially if a stain is used – adversely affecting the finish and spoiling the appearance. Remove all pencil marks (a pencil eraser is often more effective than abrasive paper) and then sand clean, using the smoothest grit abrasive paper available. It is important to sand with the grain and not across it. For big jobs a power sander is useful, but final finishing should be done by hand. Protect against excessive dust. After

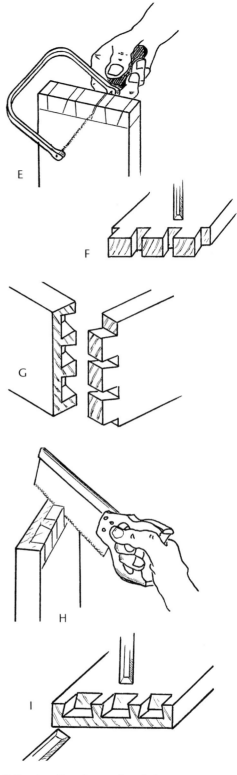

E Sawing the pins and sockets
F Cleaning up with a sharp chisel
G Lapped dovetail
H Sawing the pins and sockets
I Cleaning up the pins and sockets

sanding, wipe away the dust from the surface of the wood with a soft cloth. For a really smooth finish, moisten the wood surface with a damp cloth to 'raise the grain' and when dry sand down once more and wipe clean.

Wood fillers and sealers are often referred to in descriptions of finishing methods. Fillers are mostly based on concoctions of chalk or plaster of Paris dissolved in water or linseed oil to produce a thick paste. This is applied to wood to fill very open grain and when dry it is sanded smooth. Proprietary brands of sanding sealer are easier to use and are recommended for most circumstances. These have ethnol or shellac as a solvent and have the advantage of being quick-drying. Safe-to-use water-soluble sealers are also available.

Wood may be stained to alter or enrich its colour or to enhance the natural figure or grain pattern. There are four general types of stain: water, oil, spirit and chemical. The first, and least expensive, consists mainly of pigment or dye dissolved in water; this penetrates the wood, causing the grain to rise. Oil stains do not give rise to this problem as their colours are dissolved in turpentine or a similar substance, but they are expensive. Spirit stains consist of dry pigments in methylated spirits; they dry rapidly on contact with the wood surface and can be difficult to apply evenly; their colours also have a tendency to fade. Chemical stains work by reacting with the particular wood to which they are applied and results are therefore less predictable. As a precaution, never use any stain without first testing it. After staining, seal the surface with a coat of varnish, polish, oil or wax.

Various paints have been used to colour wood since Egyptian times. Before applying most paint finishes it is advisable to prime or seal the surface using either a suitable undercoat or a sealer such as matt polyurethane varnish. Emulsion paints dry quickly and are more or less odourless and water-soluble. They give a flat (matt) finish and are suitable only for indoor use. Gloss paint provides a harder, more durable, outdoor finish which can be wiped clean. Latex paints and acrylics are also available for application to wood. An attractive paint finish is produced by using 'milk' paint. This is a material popularized by the interest in furniture and artefacts made in the American Shaker communities. Since it is water-soluble it is pleasant to use and it dries quickly, becoming lighter in colour as it does so to leave a matt finish. When it is dry, a coat of glaze or wax polish may be added to seal and darken the surface.

Traditional varnishes contain natural gums and resins dissolved in either linseed oil or methylated spirits. These create a near-transparent finish which can be applied over bare, stained or painted wood. It acts as a preservative and provides a hard-wearing surface. Today the most popular 'varnish' is the polyurethane type, available in matt, satin or semi-matt and gloss. It is better to brush on two or three thinned coats of this material (diluted with white spirit) than one full-strength coat straight from the can.

The oldest oil finish is, of course, linseed oil. It is simple to apply and gives a durable, near-transparent finish, moderately resistant to moisture and heat. Its disadvantage is that it requires several applications and each must dry before the next is applied. More modern formulations, such as Danish oil and both tung and teak oil, incorporate rapid-drying agents and these are now more commonly used. They are applied in much the same way as linseed oil with a brush or with a cloth. An added advantage of all oil finishes – and of wax too – is that they are easily renewable.

Beeswax is an equally old and much-used finish and, mixed with turpentine and small amounts of other 'secret' ingredients, is today sold under a variety of proprietary names. Avoid cheap wax polishes – they usually include paraffin wax – and do not use those containing silicon. Some wax polishes are said to be suitable for application to bare wood, but I would recommend the initial use of a sealer to avoid the disappointment of uneven penetration and distribution. Smooth the sealer before waxing and apply the wax on a soft cloth. Leave to dry for a few minutes then buff up with a clean, soft, dry cloth. Wax may also be applied over an oil finish to good effect.

Various techniques can be used to simulate the effect of age and wear on a piece of furniture. Generally known as 'distressing', these tricks are widely practised and have now become more accepted, providing they are not used to fake new pieces as 'genuine' old ones. Before any stain or finish is applied, it is possible to 'age' wood by denting and scratching surfaces, and chipping and rounding over edges to give the appearance of extensive use. Further age and use effects can be achieved by applying stain or paint and then partially removing it before applying another finish such as wax. Commercially produced 'old pine' stain will conveniently age most softwoods, while thinned grey paint brushed on and wiped off will give a traditional limed finish to most hardwoods, especially oak. Antique waxes – wax polishes containing darkening pigments – applied to both softwoods and hardwoods will quickly impart a desirable patina. Paint finishes can be artificially aged using special 'crackle' varnish or by applying patches of wax polish before painting which causes the paint to flake off, simulating the effects of dampness and old age.

All these ageing effects require restraint if they are to look convincing. Simulate wear where it would occur in normal use; it would be most in evidence in areas such as around door handles and on chair rails and table legs. Dirt and dust would accumulate only in certain places such as recesses in deep mouldings. Avoid making the distressed finish too artificial-looking.

PART TWO

Projects

Wall Shelf with Drawer

Wall-mounted shelves for storing or perhaps
displaying all manner of household
odds and ends were once very common and they
still serve a useful purpose in the
homes of today. This simple design makes
an ideal first project either for
personal use or as a gift.

***Introduction** It is difficult for us fully to appreciate, with our built-in cupboards, fully fitted bathrooms and wall-to-wall kitchen cabinets, just how useful and how widely used simple, wall-hung shelves and cupboards were in the past. Small shelves, such as the one described here, could be found in any room in the house – in the kitchen one might be used for small cooking utensils, cook books or perhaps spices; in the bathroom for toiletries; in the living room for small artefacts; and elsewhere used to store medicines and so on. The design is traditional, the shaped sides giving rise to the descriptive name waterfall front.

Wall-hung shelves come in all shapes and sizes, some without drawers, others with one drawer or more; others, like this one, have a back, others do not. The occupants of both English country houses and American Shaker communities found them equally useful.

***Construction Details** The straightforward construction of this small shelf with drawer makes it an ideal first project. The material requirements are quite small and the described method requires only simple housing joints and some grooving and rebating, all of which can be done by hand or perhaps with the help of a power router. The drawer construction, as described, utilizes a rebated joint which is easy to make and gives quite satisfactory results. However, if a dovetailed drawer is preferred, this remains an option. Furthermore, the overall dimensions can easily be altered to suit individual requirements. To hang the shelves on the wall a mirror plate screwed to the back at the level of the top shelf and a substantial screw in the wall are adequate.

Cutting List *(Add waste)*			
No.	Item	in	mm
2	Sides	$18 \times 7 \times 5/8$	$457 \times 178 \times 16$
2	Bottom shelves	$12^{1}/_{2} \times 7 \times 5/8$	$318 \times 178 \times 16$
1	Top shelf	$12^{1}/_{2} \times 3^{1}/_{2} \times 5/8$	$318 \times 89 \times 16$
1	Back	$19 \times 12 \times 3/8$	$483 \times 305 \times 10$
1	Drawer front	$12 \times 3^{1}/_{2} \times 5/8$	$305 \times 89 \times 16$
2	Drawer sides	$6^{1}/_{2} \times 3^{1}/_{2} \times 1/2$	$165 \times 89 \times 13$
1	Drawer back	$12 \times 2^{3}/_{4} \times 1/2$	$305 \times 70 \times 13$
1	Drawer bottom	$11^{1}/_{2} \times 6 \times 1/4$	$292 \times 152 \times 6$

Material Pine or any suitable hardwood.

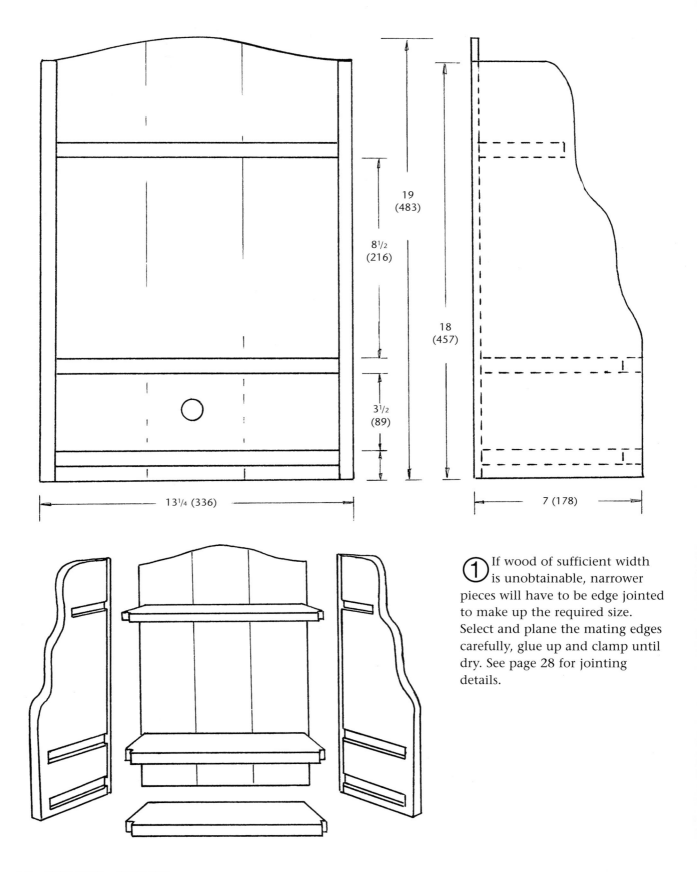

19
(483)

8¹/₂
(216)

18
(457)

3¹/₂
(89)

13¹/₄ (336)

7 (178)

① If wood of sufficient width is unobtainable, narrower pieces will have to be edge jointed to make up the required size. Select and plane the mating edges carefully, glue up and clamp until dry. See page 28 for jointing details.

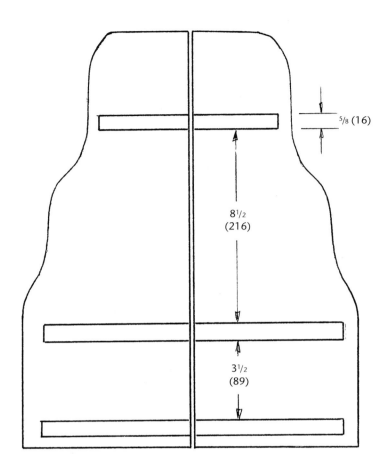

$^{5}/_{8}$ (16)

$8^{1}/_{2}$
(216)

$3^{1}/_{2}$
(89)

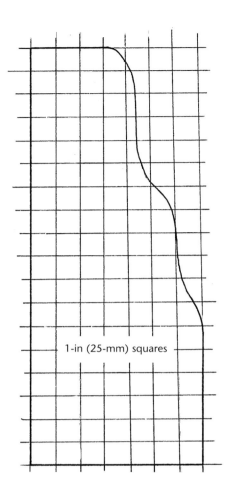

1-in (25-mm) squares

② Begin by cutting the two side pieces to length and mark out and cut them to the prescribed shape. Then mark out the position of the housing joints for the shelves. The joint used is the stopped housing or dado; details of this simple joint are given on page 31. Mark out and cut the housings as described. Marking out as a pair as shown ensures that the housings are equally spaced on both pieces.

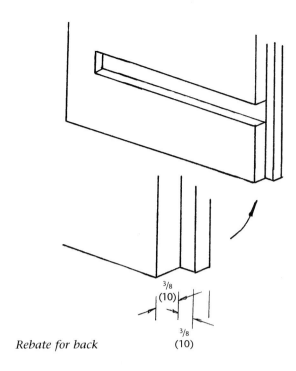

Rebate for back

$\frac{3}{8}$
(10)

$\frac{3}{8}$
(10)

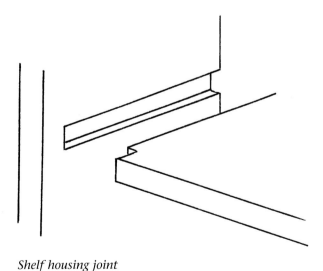

Shelf housing joint

3 Make the rebate on the back inside edge of each side piece to accommodate the back when fitted. This may easily be done by hand using a rebate plane and even more easily using a power router and suitable cutter.

4 Cut the three shelves, two of equal width, one narrower, to exactly equal length and square across the ends. Cut out the notch at the front to match up with the stopped housing. Try each shelf in its respective housing to obtain a good fit. Trim a shaving off the bottom of each shelf if necessary.

5 Mark out and cut the side pieces to the prescribed shape. Clean up and smooth the sawn edges. Clean up all surfaces, removing any unwanted marks. Have a trial or dry assembly – that is, without glue – to be sure that everything goes together correctly. Cramp up and check for squareness, paying particular attention to the drawer opening. When satisfactory, disassemble and prepare for gluing.

6 Put sufficient glue into each housing – but don't overdo it, leaving a lot to clean off later; put the corresponding shelf into position and cramp up. Check again for squareness. Clean off any surplus glue and leave until set and dry.

⑦ The back consists of narrow pieces, ideally tongued and grooved or rebated. Put these in 'loose' – that is, without gluing – to hide the effects of any shrinkage which may occur. Arrange the pieces to fit equally across the back and into the rebated side pieces. Before fitting, mark out the curved top; fit together all the individual back pieces and then saw them to shape. Hold the back in place by means of small panel pins along the rebate and across the back of the shelves.

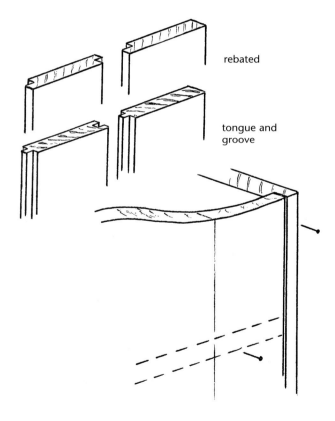

rebated

tongue and groove

Alternative back pieces and fixing method

⑧ The drawer may be made with dovetail joints – lapped at the front, through at the back (see page 38 for dovetail jointing details) – or it can be made more easily using a plain glued and pinned rebated joint as shown. This is a simple but satisfactory method of drawer making for small work of this kind.

⑨ First, cut a drawer front slightly oversize and plane it to be a good fit in the drawer opening. Cut and plane the two side pieces to the same width and to the required length; cut the back piece about the same length as the drawer front and about $5/8$ in (16 mm) narrower. Note that the two side pieces are of thinner material than the drawer front while the back piece, thinner still, is the same thickness as the drawer bottom.

⑩ Rebate the front piece to the thickness of the side pieces, with a lap of $1/8$ in (3 mm) left at the front. Cut a groove along the inside bottom edge to provide a slot for the drawer bottom. Groove the two side pieces similarly for the same purpose – the three grooves must of course align correctly with each other. Also make a groove across the back inside end of each side piece to hold the back piece in place. This will need trimming to length to fit. Clean off all unwanted marks and prepare to assemble the drawer.

Drawer construction

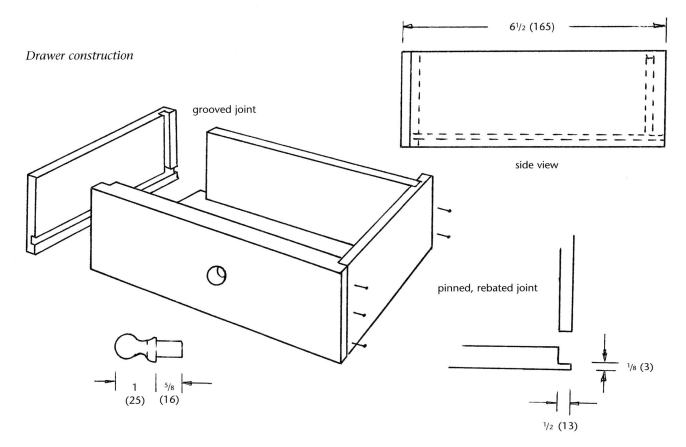

grooved joint

6¹/₂ (165)

side view

pinned, rebated joint

¹/₈ (3)

¹/₂ (13)

1 (25)   ⁵/₈ (16)

⑪ Assemble the drawer by gluing and panel pinning the sides into their respective rebates. Glue the back into the grooves made for it and position it so that the drawer bottom, when fitted, passes under it. Cramp up, check for squareness and leave to dry. Then trim the bottom to size and slide it into the grooves made to accommodate it. Do not glue in the drawer bottom, but pin it where it passes below the back. Ease the drawer if necessary to a nice sliding fit. Turn or purchase a small knob and fit this correctly to the drawer front.

⑫ If pine is used, the shelf may be painted and perhaps given a distressed look, or it may be clear finished as this one was. A clear finish should also be the choice if an attractive hardwood is used. See page 39 for finishing techniques.

Corner Cupboard

Corner cupboards are extremely useful in filling what may often be an awkward part of a room – unless, of course, you live in a converted windmill or lighthouse. Furthermore they are quite suitable for any part of the home – just let your imagination run free.

Introduction Corner cupboards provide a satisfactory answer to the problem of how to make the best use of awkward parts of a room. Known from the seventeenth century, early examples were frequently built-in pieces of furniture matched to the wainscot or wood panelling of the room. Later, as buildings and fashion changed and panelled walls gave way to plaster and paint and, later still, to wallpaper, they became separate pieces of furniture. Initially used for a wide range of purposes including the storage of food and all kinds of household items, these three-cornered cupboards continued to have solid, panelled doors and it was not until the display of precious possessions became popular that glazed doors were introduced.

Some corner cupboards were as tall as the room was high and stood on the floor, while others were two-tiered and placed one on top of the other. Many, such as the one described here, were made as a single piece to fit to the wall, and these are often described as hanging cupboards. They were made in a variety of woods: oak and later mahogany were both used and pine was popular too.

Construction Details In this design, which was constructed by Tim Boxley, one of my City and Guilds students, when he was seventeen years of age, I have departed from the usual method of forming the 45-degree turn at each of the front corners by means of a rather elaborate construction of separate angled pieces joined by loose tongues glued into their mating edges. Instead, the single stile at each front corner has two 45-degree bevels planed on it, one of which forms one side of the door opening. This, together with the use of identical triangular pieces, which form top, bottom and shelves, greatly simplifies the construction of this piece of furniture.

Cutting List (Add waste)			
No.	Item	in	mm
1	Door panel	28 × 14 × 1/2	711 × 356 × 13
2	Side panels	30 × 14 × 1/2	762 × 356 × 13
2	Shelf pieces	35 × 12 × 1/2	889 × 305 × 13
2	Front stiles	30 × 3³/4 × 1¹/2	762 × 95 × 38
2	Front rails	18¹/2 × 1³/4 × ³/4	470 × 44 × 19
1	Back post	30 × 3³/4 × 1	762 × 95 × 25
1	Shelf bearer piece	24 × 1/2 × 1/2	610 × 13 × 13
2	Door stiles	27 × 1³/4 × ³/4	686 × 44 × 19
2	Door rails	15 × 1³/4 × ³/4	381 × 44 × 19
1	Pediment	26 × 3 × 1/2	660 × 76 × 13

Material Pine, cherry, beech or oak.

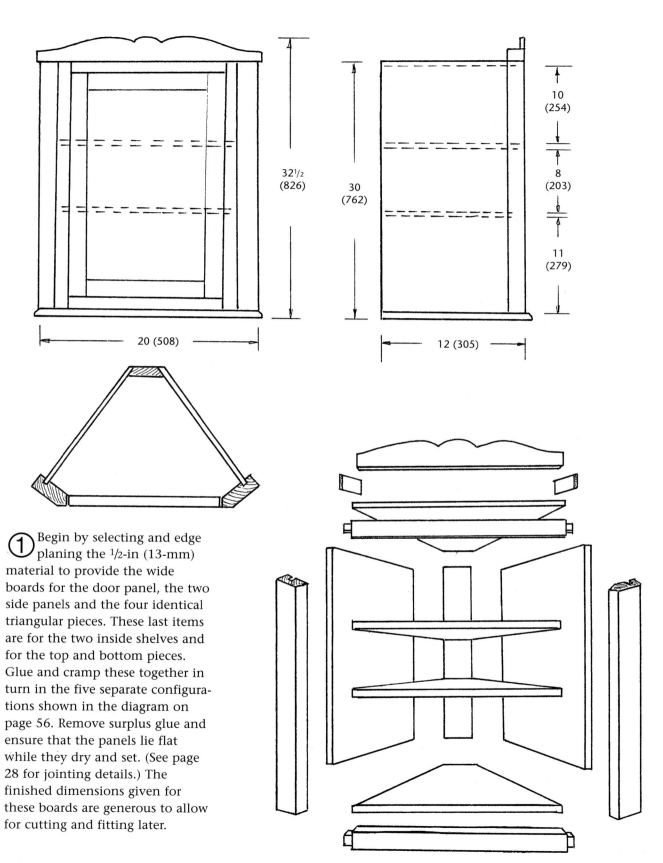

32¹/₂
(826)

20 (508)

10
(254)

8
(203)

11
(279)

30
(762)

12 (305)

① Begin by selecting and edge planing the ¹/₂-in (13-mm) material to provide the wide boards for the door panel, the two side panels and the four identical triangular pieces. These last items are for the two inside shelves and for the top and bottom pieces. Glue and cramp these together in turn in the five separate configurations shown in the diagram on page 56. Remove surplus glue and ensure that the panels lie flat while they dry and set. (See page 28 for jointing details.) The finished dimensions given for these boards are generous to allow for cutting and fitting later.

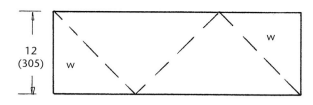

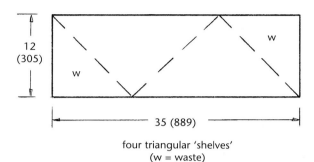

12
(305)

12
(305)

w   w

w   w

35 (889)

four triangular 'shelves'
(w = waste)

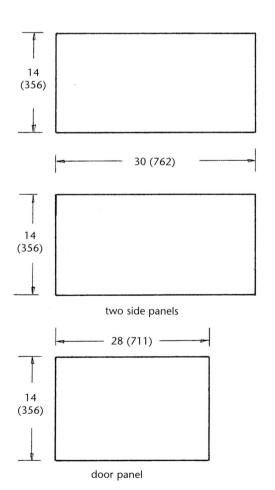

14
(356)

30 (762)

14
(356)

two side panels

28 (711)

14
(356)

door panel

② While these are drying, work on the two front stiles. First plane to size if necessary, then cut a groove to accommodate a side panel in each piece using either a hand method or a power router. Make a $^7/_{16}$-in- (11-mm)-wide groove to give a tight fit to the planed edge of each panel when fitted; the groove should be $^3/_8$ in (10 mm) deep. Next mark a centre line down the front edge of each side and carefully plane each adjacent side to the required 45-degree bevel.

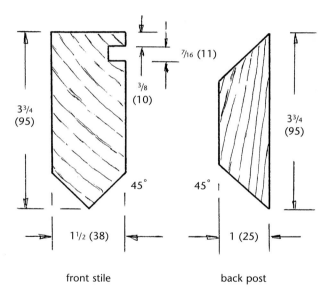

3¾
(95)

$^7/_{16}$ (11)

$^3/_8$
(10)

45°   45°

1½ (38)   1 (25)

3¾
(95)

front stile   back post

③ The back post has its two opposite edges chamfered to 45 degrees also and this can be done at this stage. To simplify and strengthen the construction further the back post is not grooved for the side panels; instead these overlie the two planed chamfers of the post and are screwed into position.

④ Now make the mortises for the two front rails in the two front stiles. Mark them out on the inside bevelled faces of each stile, as shown. Cut them out square to their marked surface and parallel to what is in effect the front edge of the cupboard. Cut them carefully to a depth of a little over 1 in (25 mm).

⑤ Then cut the two rails, top and bottom, to equal length; check the total length – it should be shoulder length, 16 in (406 mm), plus 2 in (50 mm) for the tenons, a total of 18 in (457 mm). Mark out the tenons and saw them to size. (See page 32 for jointing details.) Test fit individual tenons into their respective mortises, trim to fit as necessary; mark mating pieces for identification purposes and put aside until later.

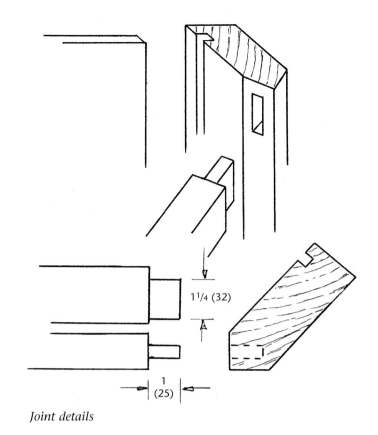

1¼ (32)

1 (25)

Joint details

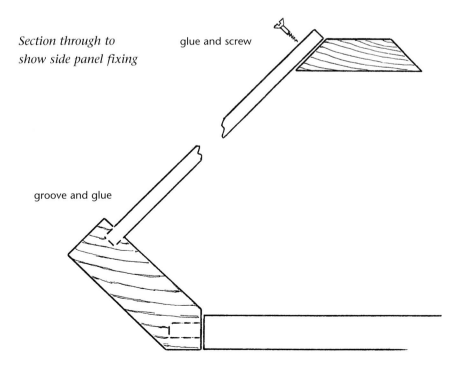

Section through to show side panel fixing

glue and screw

groove and glue

⑥ Now cut to size the wide board glued up to make the two side panels; the finished measurement of each should be 30 × 13 in (762 × 330 mm) and they must be 'square'. Plane or spokeshave one long back edge of each panel to be a good fit in the grooves already cut in the front stiles and at the opposite edge drill three clearance holes for the no. 8 screws used to fix the panels to the back post. Countersink these holes on the outside face and check the panels for fit in their respective grooves.

(7) Next mark out and cut to shape the glued-up, wide boards for the four triangular pieces. This is economically done as shown in the diagrams on page 56 (top left). To achieve the final size and shape I used a template made as shown below – always handy when doing repetitive work and I would recommend this method even when marking only four of a kind as in this case. The pattern is purposely a little oversize to allow for trimming to fit your cupboard during assembly so as to give a good fit on completion.

(8) The carcass is now ready for a 'dry assembly' – that is, without glue. Working with the cupboard components in an upright position on the bench, fit top and bottom front rails to the front stiles and add the side panels, ensuring that they go all the way and evenly into their grooves. Now put the back post in position and screw the panels into place. Pull everything together with a pair of webbing cramps or similar. If the mortise-and-tenon joints between front stiles and rails are well made and tight and the side panels are snug in their grooves, there should be no problems.

(9) With everything held correctly together, check the fit of the triangular pieces one by one. Each should be a nice push fit into the assembled carcass – trim where necessary to achieve this. They will be held in place on small wooden bearers. This method greatly simplifies construction and assembly. Ascertain and mark the position of each piece, choosing the location of the two shelves to suit your own requirements. Note that the bottom piece lies flush with the top of the bottom rail, the top piece flush with the top of the side panels. Identify each of the triangular pieces so that they re-assemble correctly.

Shelf template

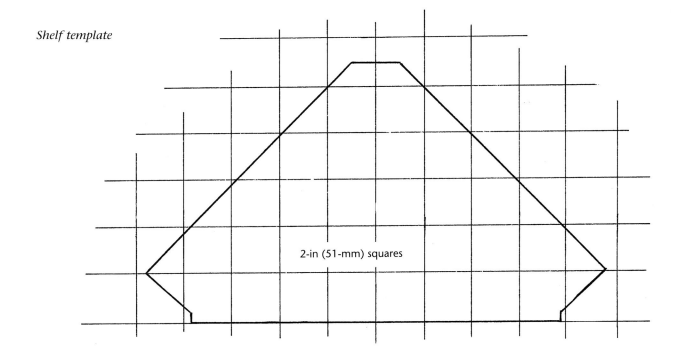

2-in (51-mm) squares

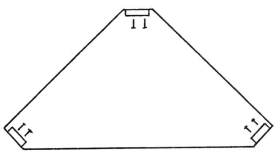

shelf bearer positions

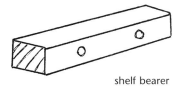

shelf bearer

⑩ Prepare the small bearers by marking the 24 × ½ × ½-in (610 × 13 × 13-mm) piece into twelve pieces each 2 in (51 mm) long, and before sawing drill two clearance holes for no. 4 screws in each marked piece. Then saw into separate parts.

⑪ Disassemble the 'dry-run' carcass. Clean off the inevitable finger and tool marks and unwanted pencil marks. It is useful at this stage to screw the shelf and top and bottom bearers into position without glue and them remove them. (The triangular pieces cannot be easily fitted during final assembly with all the bearers in place, but this pre-screwing makes their fitting after the carcass is assembled much easier.)

⑫ Begin the final assembly by gluing and joining up the top and bottom front rails with the front stiles. Then glue the side panels into the grooves in the back of each stile – push the panels in to full depth – and add the back post by gluing and screwing. Pull everything together with webbing cramps or whatever you used before and clean off any surplus glue. Place the front down on a protected level surface, push two of the triangular pieces inside the carcass to keep it in shape and leave until the glue is dry and set.

⑬ When the carcass can be handled, screw the small bearers back into place and fit the triangular pieces. Begin with the bottom piece, then add each shelf in turn and finally fix in the top. The top and bottom pieces should be screwed down for added security, but the intermediate shelves may be left loose.

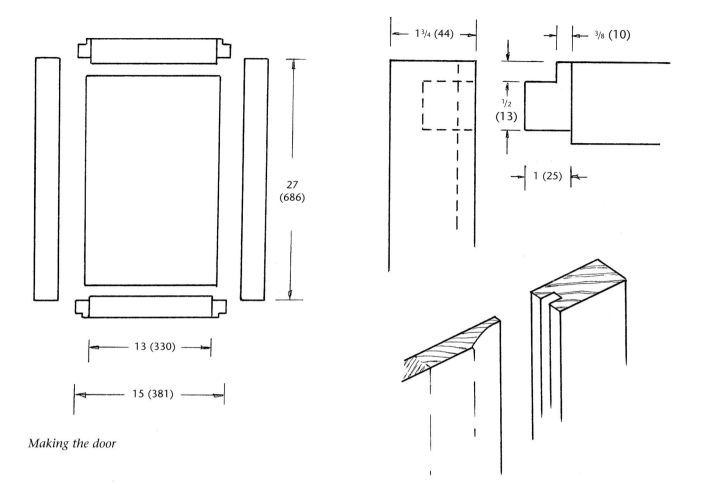

Making the door

⑭ Now start to construct the door. Although dimensions are given, it is best to take exact measurements from the opening in your cupboard – they may be slightly different. Use those given only as a guide. The door frame has haunched mortise-and-tenons and the groove which accommodates the door panel is ¼ in (6mm) wide and ⅜ in (10 mm) deep. See page 32 for jointing and page 34 for grooving details.

⑮ First cut the door frame components to length; be generous and make a very slightly oversize door which can be trimmed to fit. Now cut the groove on the inside edge of all four pieces. Mark out and cut the mortises in the upright stiles, then mark out and cut the haunched tenons in the top and bottom rails. (The haunch effectively fills in the end of the groove visible at the end of each stile.) Try individual joints for a good fit and trim as necessary. Assemble the frame without glue and check that it is square.

⑯ With the door frame assembled, ascertain the required size of the door panel by carefully measuring the inside space, then add ½ in (13 mm) to each dimension to be accommodated in the groove – ¼ in (6 mm) for each opposite side. Mark out the panel, ensure that it is square and cut to size. Plane a long chamfer on each back edge to fit into the groove in the door frame. Disassemble the door frame and try individual edges of the panel for a good fit, which should be neat but free to move. Have a dry assembly of frame and panel to ensure that everything goes together, then disassemble and clean off unwanted marks.

17 Assemble the door by gluing the mortise-and-tenons, but leave the panel unglued to allow for movement. Cramp up, clean off any surplus glue and check for squareness and twist, then leave until the glue is dry and set. Trim the door to a good, neat fit in the door opening and when satisfied hang the door on a pair of good butt hinges and fit a suitable knob and an inside catch if required.

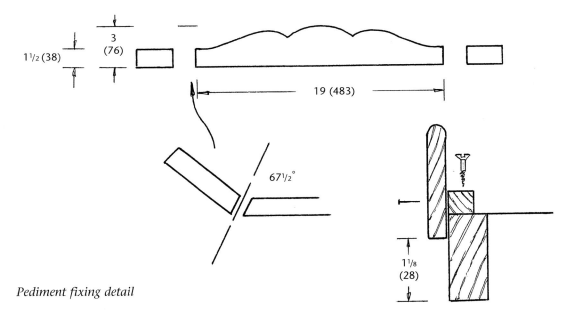

Pediment fixing detail

18 Finally, cut to size and fit the pediment which goes atop the cupboard. This can be to any design of your choice provided it is within the overal dimensions given. Cut the mitres at 67½ degrees to turn the corner correctly. The pediment is overlaid as shown in the diagram and held in place by blocks glued and screwed to the top of the cupboard. The narrow moulding placed around the bottom edge completes the job. Its mitred corners are also cut at 67½ degrees.

19 The completed cupboard may be finished in a variety of ways. It could be clear finished with sanding sealer followed by wax polish or, if intended for a bathroom or kitchen, given two or three coats of thinned-down satin polyurethane. Alternatively it could be painted, as early pine furniture was. See page 39 for advice on finishing.

Tripod Table

Perfect for country-style afternoon teas,

this elegant table was made of

timber from the cherry tree. With a top which

revolves and tilts, so that it can be

conveniently placed against a

wall when not in use, it will look good

made in any wood.

Introduction The tripod table became fashionable around the middle of the eighteenth century, probably because of the increasing popularity of afternoon tea as a socially acceptable pastime, especially for ladies. A diminutive form of the larger, circular dining table, the tripod type generally had the advantage that its top revolved and tipped up so that it could, when not in use, be conveniently placed against a wall or in a corner. In the latter case, if one leg were positioned towards the corner, the table could be quite unobtrusive. In the tilted position a table with a nicely figured top was also distinctly decorative. While the main support of the table is a single turned pillar or pedestal, the name tripod table is a reference to the three spreading feet or legs – a form of support which dates back to the ancient Greeks who recognized that anything supported at three points is stable, even on an uneven surface. The tops vary widely in these tables, from the elaborate tray with fretted gallery of the Chippendale period, to those with 'pie-crust' edging or ornate octagonal shape, to the plain, country-made circle as described here.

Construction Details Made by one of my City and Guilds students, Tim Boxley, when he was eighteen, this table incorporates a simple tilting-top mechanism known as a 'birdcage' (a 'crow's nest' in the USA). It consists of two square pieces of wood joined together at each corner by a stout, turned pillar. Both pieces of wood are drilled out to accommodate a turned shank on the supporting pillar. A short wedge through the shank holds it in place while allowing the birdcage to revolve and the top is attached so that it can be tilted. The supporting pillar incorporates sliding dovetail housings which joint the three legs or feet to it – these must be made with care to be successful.

Cutting List (Add waste)			
No.	Item	in	mm
1	Top (to make)	$23 \times 23 \times {}^{7}/_{8}$	$584 \times 584 \times 22$
1	Turned column	$20 \times 3^{1}/_{2} \times 3^{1}/_{2}$	$508 \times 89 \times 89$
3	Legs (from)	$10 \times 8 \times 1^{1}/_{2}$	$254 \times 203 \times 38$
2	Battens	$18 \times 2 \times 1$	$457 \times 51 \times 25$
2	Birdcage pieces	$5 \times 5 \times {}^{3}/_{4}$	$127 \times 127 \times 19$
4	Birdcage pillars	$4 \times 1 \times 1$	$102 \times 25 \times 25$
1	Wedge	$4 \times 1^{1}/_{2} \times {}^{1}/_{2}$	$102 \times 38 \times 13$

Material Cherry, beech, oak or pine.

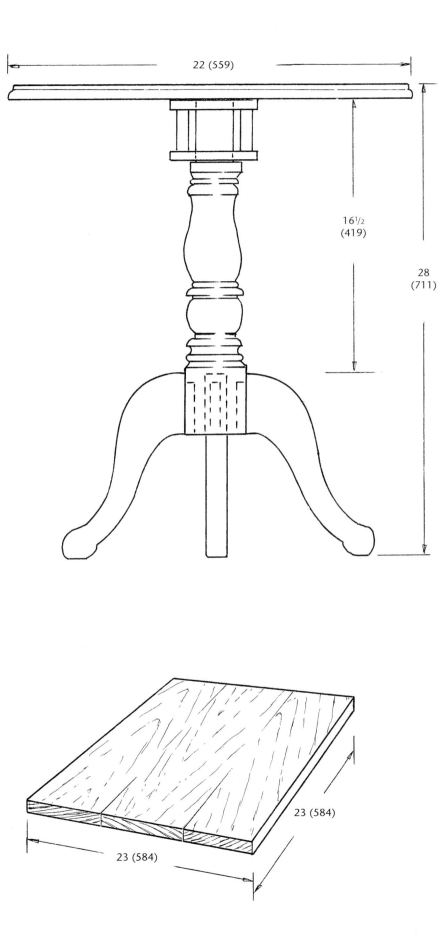

22 (559)

16½ (419)

28 (711)

23 (584)

23 (584)

1. Make up material for the top by edge jointing narrow boards together. Select pieces matching in figure and colour and, after careful planing, glue these together and leave in cramps to set and dry (see page 28 for further details).

2. Now turn the centre column. First reduce it to a 3½-in-(89-mm)-diameter cylinder, then mark out as in the diagram. The plain untouched area at the bottom will later accommodate the three legs, while the reduced shank at the top will be fitted into the tilting mechanism (the birdcage) under the top.

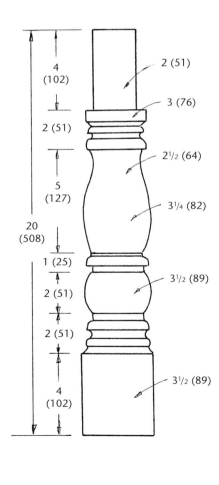

4 (102)

2 (51)

5 (127)

20 (508)

1 (25)

2 (51)

2 (51)

4 (102)

2 (51)

3 (76)

2½ (64)

3¼ (82)

3½ (89)

3½ (89)

③ Cut the legs as shown in the diagram. To ensure uniformity it is advisable to make a template by scaling up the drawn shape. Place the template on the wood so that best advantage is taken of the grain direction to maximize strength. Each leg is subsequently shaped, but first the dovetail joints which join them to the column must be marked out, then carefully cut and fitted.

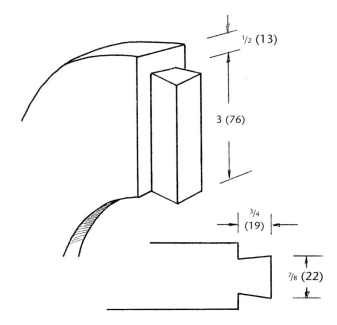

Sliding dovetail detail

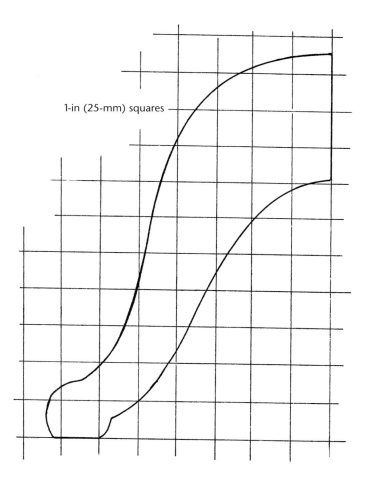

1-in (25-mm) squares

Leg template

④ Mark out and cut the joint as shown in the diagram. Note that it is slightly tapered along its length; the purpose is that if a long sliding joint such as this were parallel all the way it would be held too tightly as soon as it entered its socket from below. With both dovetail and socket tapered the joint does not start to tighten until it is almost fully 'home'. If the joint became too tight too soon and had to be forced into place, splitting would almost certainly occur. Equally, the joint must not be too loose a fit – therefore the joint, to be successful, must be carefully made and trimmed to size.

⑤ First, mark out and cut the long dovetails on the upper end of each leg. Refer to the diagram.

6 Establish the location of each leg where it abuts the column and make the contact areas flat before marking out the required sockets. Divide the plain turned base of the column into three and mark parallel lines spaced 120 degrees apart on the column; mark two further lines, 1 in (25 mm) either side, to delineate the 2-in- (51-mm)-wide flat area and level this by careful chiselling and planing until it is smooth. The dovetail sockets are worked out central to each flat area (at 120 degrees). Some wood-workers advocate using the indi-vidual dovetail already cut on the legs as templates held against the base of the column. Cut the sockets into the base of the column as shown by careful sawing and chiselling. Maintain the slight taper towards the top. Test fit each leg individually into its socket and mark the corre-sponding parts for ease of identi-fication later. Avoid making too many test fits as this can cause the joint to become too loose.

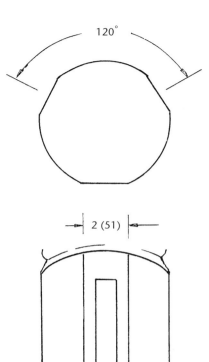

Dovetail socket on bottom of centre column

7 Complete the legs by shaping and smoothing them using spokeshave and abrasives. Round over all the edges, removing suf-ficient material to lighten their appearance without losing strength. Some antique examples are much reduced and, while this makes them quite elegant, they are not very strong in regular use.

Detail showing birdcage and spring catch with lock plate

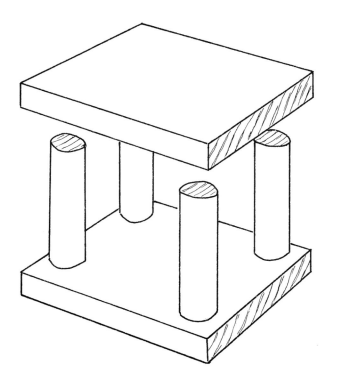

⑧ The tilting mechanism, or birdcage, at the opposite end of the centre column consists of rectangular top and bottom pieces joined by four turned pillars or posts which fit and are glued into holes drilled into them. The top and bottom pieces of the birdcage each have a 2-in (51-mm) hole drilled through their centre to accept the reduced shank at the top of the column. Make these two holes before assembling the birdcage and do it by temporarily sandwiching the top and bottom pieces together and cutting the two holes simultaneously so that they register exactly. They should be a snug fit on the column shank.

Making the birdcage

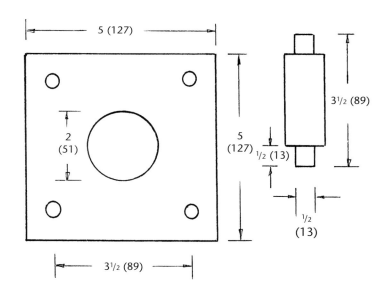

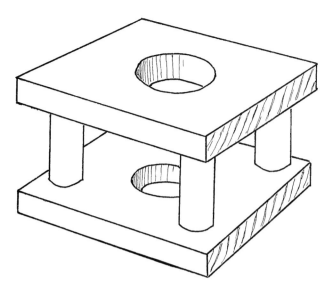

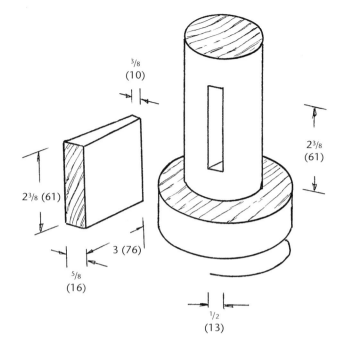

Details of birdcage construction

3/8 (10)

2³/8 (61) (square piece)

3 (76)

5/8 (16)

2³/8 (61)

1/2 (13)

⑨ After making the birdcage parts, assemble them as shown. The birdcage will subsequently be attached to the table top in a manner which allows it to tilt (see below). It is held on the column by means of a wooden wedge which acts as a retaining pin while allowing the top to be rotated. A slot is cut through the shank to take the wedge; mark the position of this with the birdcage in place so that the bottom of the wedge slot corresponds to the top surface of the bottom member of the birdcage. Make a tapered wedge and ensure that its length is within the confines of the four support posts when turned.

⑩ With column, legs and tilting mechanism completed, attention should now turn to the top of the table. Saw a generous 22-in- (559-mm)-diameter circle from the board prepared earlier and either smooth and round over the sawn edge by hand or work a simple moulding on it – use an electric router, which, with the aid of a suitable jig, could also cut the circle in the first place. Alternatively turn it on a lathe if this working capacity is available. Clean up the top surface by light planing and scraping.

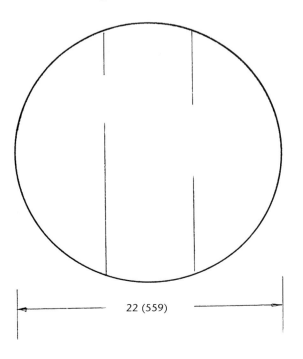

22 (559)

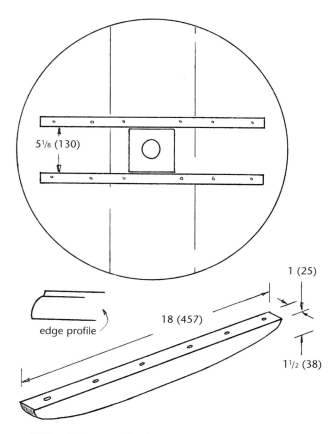

5 1/8 (130)

1 (25)

18 (457)

1 1/2 (38)

edge profile

Fitting battens under top

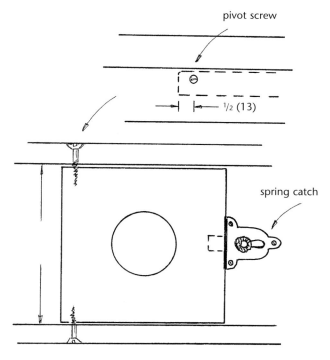

pivot screw

1/2 (13)

spring catch

Fixing top to birdcage

11 Fix battens, or cleats, underneath the top across the grain of the wood. These strengthen the top and are also strategically placed so that they act as bearers for the tilting arrangement. Positioned with their inside faces a fraction over 2 1/2 in (64 mm) either side of the centre line, they just give clearance to the top part of the birdcage to which they are attached, offset as shown, by means of brass screws. Attach the battens to the table top, unglued, by slot screwing to allow for any movement of the wood. Screw cups under the heads of the two brass pivot screws will ease the tilting movement. Fit a suitable spring catch and lock plate, sometimes known as a banjo catch, to the opposite side to lock the top in the up position.

12 After one final test to ensure that all goes together correctly, disassemble and clean up the separate components, removing all unwanted marks and so on. Then glue the legs into the column, remove any surplus glue and leave to dry and set. After this it is a matter of attaching the birdcage to the column by means of the wedge and the top to the birdcage by the two brass screws. Check that the spring catch is correctly fitted and that its locking action is positive: this is very important.

13 The finish applied to the complete table will be influenced by its use; a wax-polished finish would suit its intended purpose – that is, in a living room or hall. But if it were used in a kitchen, a finish less susceptible to dampness and spillage would probably be more appropriate. (See page 39 for finishing details.)

Pot-board Dresser

A departure from the ubiquitous Welsh dresser,
this useful piece of furniture is a
return to the original development from side
table with separate shelves above.
Entirely functional, the pot-board dresser
also provides the ideal setting for the display
of your favourite collectables.

Introduction The pot-board dresser evolved from the separate medieval side-board and cup-board and the name dresser probably came from the Norman French *dressoire,* a side table (or *borde* in the language spoken in England at the time of the conquest) on which food was prepared or 'dressed' prior to being served at the table. During the sixteenth century and later a frieze and then drawers were added below the table top and under the influence of later designs and the dictates of fashion sideboards and dressers became very ornate and pretentious. In the country cottage, however, the plain 'table' base, often with a separate plate rack fixed to the wall above, continued in favour. In due course this too changed, becoming a shelved upper section placed directly on to the base, and with the addition of enclosing cupboard doors below we have the kitchen dresser, generally known as the Welsh dresser, with which we are familiar today.

These cupboarded dressers have completely altered the traditional table-like construction to a framed carcass and in so doing have lost much of their original charm. The design outlined below is a return to the open table base, correctly called a pot-board dresser on account of the low board or shelf upon which large pots were kept. The upper section incorporates a small cupboard in which spices and other items would have been stored, often under lock and key.

Construction Details The method of construction is traditional with some minor changes to ease assembly. By securing the front and back mortise-and-tenon joints in the lower section with pegs, properly done by the draw boring method (see page 35), the need to use long sash cramps is avoided as the pegs will effectively pull the joints up tight. Similarly, the upper section is put together so that a rigid frame which resists any sideways pull is achieved. The upper sections may be located in position on the base on short loose dowels and the rest left to weight and gravity. Alternatively, fixing plates screwed across at the back could be used to join the two parts together.

No.	Item	in	mm
	Cutting List (Add waste)		
	LOWER SECTION CARCASS		
5	Legs	$32 \times 2^{3}/_{4} \times 2^{3}/_{4}$	$813 \times 70 \times 70$
1	Front top rail	$43^{1}/_{2} \times 1^{1}/_{2} \times {}^{3}/_{4}$	$1105 \times 38 \times 19$
1	Front apron	$43^{1}/_{2} \times 5 \times {}^{3}/_{4}$	$1105 \times 127 \times 19$
1	Back top rail	$43^{1}/_{2} \times 10 \times {}^{3}/_{4}$	$1105 \times 254 \times 19$
2	Side top rails	$14^{1}/_{2} \times 10 \times {}^{3}/_{4}$	$369 \times 254 \times 19$
2	Drawer dividers	$6 \times 2 \times {}^{3}/_{4}$	$152 \times 51 \times 19$
2	Front bottom rails	$21^{1}/_{2} \times 2 \times {}^{3}/_{4}$	$546 \times 51 \times 19$
1	Back bottom rail	$43^{1}/_{2} \times 2 \times {}^{3}/_{4}$	$1105 \times 51 \times 19$

No.	Item	in	mm
2	Side bottom rails	$14^{1}/_{2} \times 2 \times {}^{3}/_{4}$	$369 \times 51 \times 19$
1	Pot board	$46^{1}/_{2} \times 17^{3}/_{4} \times {}^{3}/_{4}$	$1181 \times 445 \times 19$
1	Top	$48 \times 18^{1}/_{4} \times 1$	$1219 \times 464 \times 25$
	DRAWER RUNNERS, ETC.		
2	End runners	$15^{1}/_{2} \times 2 \times {}^{3}/_{4}$	$394 \times 51 \times 19$
2	Centre runners	$15^{1}/_{2} \times 3 \times {}^{3}/_{4}$	$394 \times 76 \times 19$
2	End guides	$12 \times 1^{1}/_{2} \times {}^{3}/_{4}$	$305 \times 38 \times 19$
2	Centre guides	$15^{1}/_{2} \times 2 \times {}^{3}/_{4}$	$394 \times 51 \times 19$
2	Centre bearers	$13^{1}/_{2} \times 1 \times {}^{3}/_{4}$	$343 \times 25 \times 19$
2	End kickers	$15^{1}/_{2} \times 2 \times {}^{3}/_{4}$	$394 \times 51 \times 19$
2	Centre kickers	$15^{1}/_{2} \times 3 \times {}^{3}/_{4}$	$394 \times 76 \times 19$
2	Centre kicker carriers	$16^{1}/_{2} \times 3 \times {}^{3}/_{4}$	$419 \times 76 \times 19$
	DRAWERS		
2	Drawer fronts	$15^{3}/_{4} \times 6^{1}/_{2} \times {}^{3}/_{4}$	$400 \times 165 \times 19$
1	Drawer front	$6^{1}/_{2} \times 6^{1}/_{2} \times {}^{3}/_{4}$	$165 \times 165 \times 19$
6	Drawer sides	$15^{1}/_{2} \times 6 \times {}^{1}/_{2}$	$394 \times 152 \times 19$
2	Drawer backs	$15^{1}/_{4} \times 5^{1}/_{2} \times {}^{1}/_{2}$	$387 \times 140 \times 13$
1	Drawer back	$6 \times 5^{1}/_{2} \times {}^{1}/_{2}$	$152 \times 140 \times 13$
2	Bottoms	$16 \times 14^{1}/_{2} \times {}^{1}/_{4}$	$406 \times 369 \times 6$
1	Bottom	$16 \times 5^{1}/_{4} \times {}^{1}/_{4}$	$406 \times 133 \times 6$
3	Turned knobs	$3 \times 2 \times 2$	$76 \times 51 \times 51$
	UPPER SECTION		
2	Sides	$39 \times 8 \times {}^{3}/_{4}$	$991 \times 203 \times 19$
2	Shelves	$45^{3}/_{4} \times 7^{1}/_{2} \times {}^{3}/_{4}$	$1162 \times 191 \times 19$
1	Front frieze	$45 \times 4^{1}/_{2} \times {}^{3}/_{4}$	$1143 \times 114 \times 19$
1	Top	$48 \times 8^{3}/_{4} \times {}^{3}/_{4}$	$1219 \times 222 \times 19$
1	Top moulding	$49 \times 2 \times {}^{3}/_{4}$	$1245 \times 51 \times 19$
1	Top beading	$47 \times {}^{3}/_{8} \times {}^{3}/_{8}$	$1194 \times 10 \times 10$
1	Bottom back rail	$46^{1}/_{2} \times 2 \times 1$	$1181 \times 51 \times 25$
2	Bottom plinths	$10 \times 2 \times 1$	$254 \times 51 \times 25$
2	Cupboard sides	$16 \times 7^{1}/_{2} \times {}^{3}/_{4}$	$406 \times 191 \times 25$
	CUPBOARD DOOR		
2	Door stiles	$11^{1}/_{2} \times 1^{1}/_{2} \times {}^{3}/_{4}$	$292 \times 38 \times 19$
2	Door rails	$9 \times 1^{1}/_{2} \times {}^{3}/_{4}$	$229 \times 38 \times 19$
1	Door panel	$9 \times 8 \times {}^{1}/_{4}$	$229 \times 203 \times 6$
1	Door knob	$1^{3}/_{4} \times 1 \times 1$	$44 \times 25 \times 25$

Material Cherry, oak, ash, beech or pine.

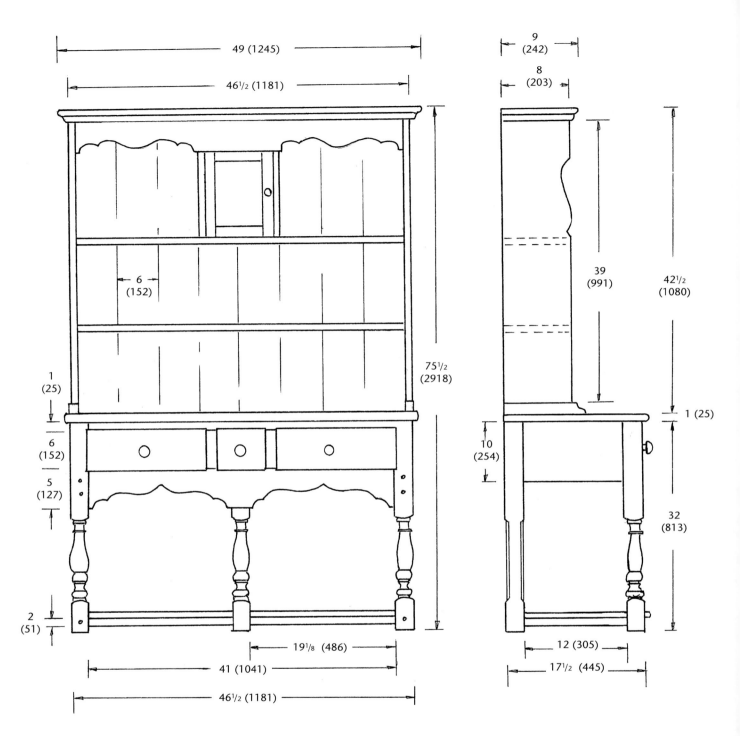

49 (1245)

46½ (1181)

9 (242)

8 (203)

6 (152)

1 (25)

6 (152)

5 (127)

2 (51)

75½ (2918)

39 (991)

42½ (1080)

1 (25)

10 (254)

32 (813)

19⅛ (486)

41 (1041)

46½ (1181)

12 (305)

17½ (445)

① Select sound, well-seasoned material, choosing the best matched and figured pieces for the major and more obvious components. Where wide pieces have to be made up by edge joining narrower pieces, prepare these first (see page 28). This applies particularly to the back and side top pieces and the top and bottom (pot board) of the lower section, the sides and top of the upper section and possibly the drawer bottoms. There are a lot of separate components, so mark them for easy identification.

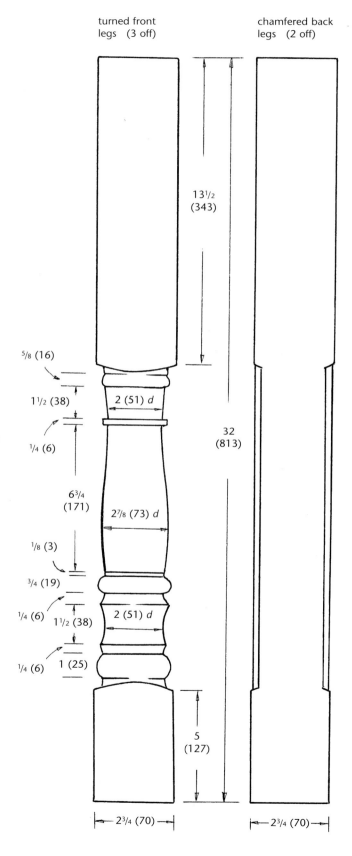

turned front
legs   (3 off)

chamfered back
legs   (2 off)

13½
(343)

32
(813)

⁵⁄₈ (16)

1½ (38)

2 (51) *d*

¼ (6)

6¾
(171)

2⁷⁄₈ (73) *d*

⅛ (3)

¾ (19)

¼ (6)

1½ (38)

2 (51) *d*

¼ (6)

1 (25)

5
(127)

2¾ (70)

2¾ (70)

②Make the lower section first. This constitutes the major part of the project, incorporating, in addition to the carcass work and jointing, turning and drawer construction. Begin with the five – yes, five – legs. Select the three front legs to be turned on the lathe; these should be cut to length initially with sufficient waste left at each end for mounting between centres on the lathe. The two back legs, which are not turned, may be cut to exact length. All five legs should now be planed square and smooth. Turn the front legs to the given design – or to any pattern of your own choice – between the designated square shoulders. Stop chamfer the two back legs between the same shoulder dimensions. Do this by carefully chiselling the stopped ends and taking out the remainder with a small plane or spokeshave. If you have no lathe, all five legs may be treated in this way.

Top corner joint details

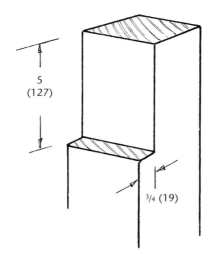

3¹/₂
(89)

6
(152)

3
(76)

1¹/₄
(32)

1¹/₄
(32)

bare-faced tenons here

Housing for drawer runners

③ Mark out the position of all the mortises in the four corner legs. (The centre front leg is fixed in differently.) Cut the mortises true and square and to the correct depth. Note the use of the double mortise and tenon on the wide back and side top pieces. (See page 35 for jointing details.) Cut the centre leg to length and cut out the top portion to accommodate the front apron.

Top of centre leg detail

5
(127)

³/₄ (19)

④ Mark out and cut the tenons on all the horizontal pieces: back, side and front bottom rails, back and side top pieces and front top rail (above the drawer opening) and front apron. (This fits below the drawer opening and requires shaping as shown in the diagram on page 78.) Note that these last two components have bare-faced tenons so that they finish flush with the front surface of the front legs. Test fit individual tenons with their respective mortises; trim to obtain a good fit. Prepare the front and back mortise-and-tenons for pegging (see page 35 for draw boring details). Make the pegs.

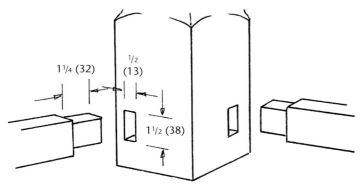

1¹/₄ (32)

¹/₂
(13)

1¹/₂ (38)

Bottom corner detail

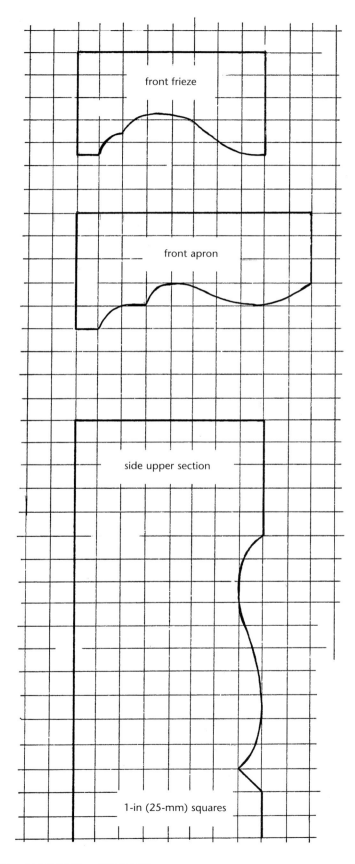

front frieze

front apron

side upper section

1-in (25-mm) squares

⑤ Now have a 'dry assembly' (without glue) of all these base or lower section components. Everything will hold together if the joints are sufficiently tight – use a pair of webbing cramps to pull things together, or sash cramps if you have them and need them. Stand the piece on a level surface and check for squareness and stability, and in particular check that the drawer opening is correct and the two long edges are parallel to avoid problems later on. While it is assembled ascertain the position and correct length of the two dividers between the drawers and make these a nice fit. (They will be dowelled and glued in place.) Then carefully locate and mark the positions for the drawer runners and kickers for each drawer.

⑥ Disassemble and first mark out and cut housings in the four corner legs to accommodate the end drawer runners and kickers. Mark out and cut the four single dovetails in the top edge of the back top piece and the front top rail for the two central drawer kicker carriers. Reaffirm the positions of the central drawer runners and screw the bearers for these into place. Cut all runners and kickers and the kicker carriers to length and drill or joint as required. Drill the front apron so that it may be screwed to the top of the centre leg.

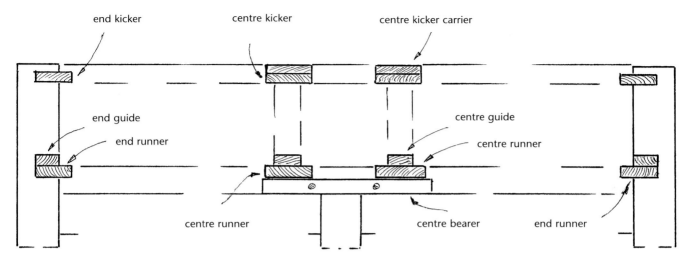

end kicker   centre kicker   centre kicker carrier

end guide

end runner

centre guide

centre runner

centre runner   centre bearer   end runner

Drawer runners, guides and kicker positions

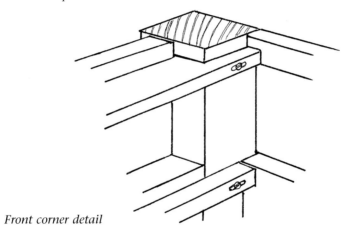

Front corner detail

⑦ Reassemble the lower section for the second time, still dry, and try all the drawer runners and kickers for a good fit. Note that these will be screwed into position without glue. This is good practice, allowing for natural movement of the wood and permitting some adjustment or replacement when worn. When everything is satisfactory, disassemble and clean up all components, removing all unwanted pencil marks and so on.

⑧ Prepare for gluing up; have cramps ready and clear the bench. Begin by gluing up the two end sections, cramp up and check that they are square and not twisted; wipe off any surplus glue and leave to dry. Glue the two front drawer dividers into place between the front top rail and the front apron and leave to dry in cramps. Do this now as it is impossible later. Then glue up the remainder of the components, assembling them in the correct sequence; first put all back and front components into one end

section, add the centre front leg and the second bottom rail and then add the other end section. Correctly position and screw the front apron to the centre front leg; drive in the pegs to secure and tighten the front and back mortise and tenon; check for squareness and stability; wipe off any surplus glue and leave to dry. Glue in the centre kicker carriers and fit the kickers. Conceal the screws holding the centre leg to the apron with false pegs; clean off all protruding pegs.

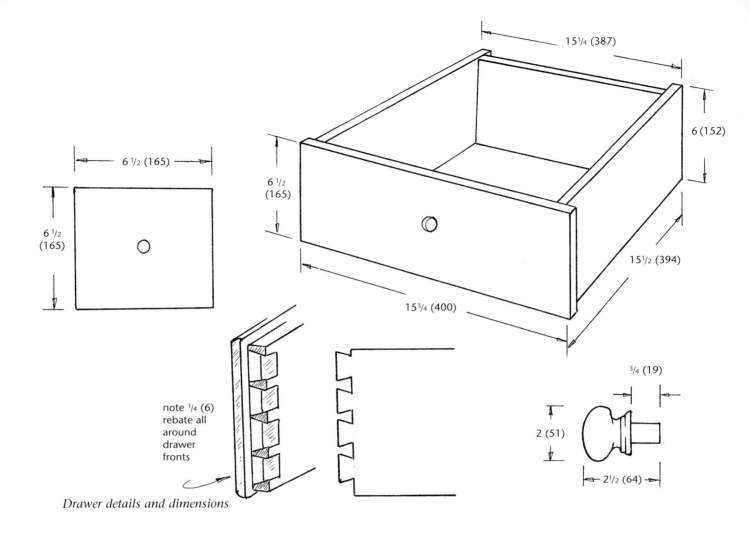

Drawer details and dimensions

Dimensions on figure:
15¼ (387)
6 (152)
6½ (165)
15½ (394)
15¾ (400)
6½ (165)
6½ (165)
note ¼ (6) rebate all around drawer fronts
¾ (19)
2 (51)
2½ (64)

9 The bottom (or pot) and top boards, made up earlier by edge jointing, can now be prepared and fitted. The bottom board rests on the bottom rails, overlapping by ½ in (13 mm) at the front and sides. Measure, mark and cut the cut-outs where it fits around the legs and fit into position. It may be held in position by screws or by nailing or pegging. The top also overlaps at the front and side. Its corners are slightly rounded to avoid a sharp point and the edges are rounded over or chamfered. The top is held in place by means of 'buttons' (see page 101), which allow for any movement that may occur.

10 Now the drawers can be made. The drawer fronts are of the rebated type, traditional in this style of furniture, designed for easy fitting and eliminating the need for drawer stops. Each drawer front is made oversize by ¼ in (6 mm) all around and rebated to fit the drawer opening. The drawer sides are individually fitted, to run tightly at first, between the drawer runners and kickers and the drawer backs are cut to size. The construction of all three drawers is identical.

11 First rebate all around the drawer front and test it for an easy fit in the drawer opening. Then make the two drawer sides a tight running fit between the runners and kickers. Mark out and cut the dovetail joints – lapped at the front, through at the back (see page 38 for joint details). Cut the grooves in each drawer side to accommodate the drawer bottom. (A piece of beading supports the drawer bottom at the front.) Assemble the drawer without glue and check for squareness. Trim to size and fit the drawer bottom; this fits into the grooves made for it, overhangs and passes under the back where it is later secured with panel pins.

12 Disassemble the drawer and clean off unwanted marks, then glue up and reassemble. Do not glue in the bottom. Cramp up and check for squareness; wipe off any surplus glue and leave to dry and set. Round over the front edges and ease individual drawers so they run more easily. Make and fit turned round wooden knobs and the drawers are finished. This completes the construction of the lower section.

13 Begin the upper section by first cutting the two side uprights to size and shape and marking out the position of the shelf housings. These are stopped housings (see page 31) and may be cut by hand or with a router. Cut the two shelves to length, notch their front ends for the stopped housing and try individually for a good fit. A round bottom groove may be run parallel to and about 1 in (25 mm) from the back edge of each shelf to provide a plate groove.

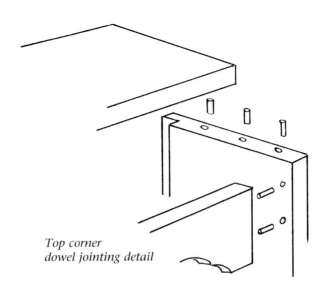

Top corner dowel jointing detail

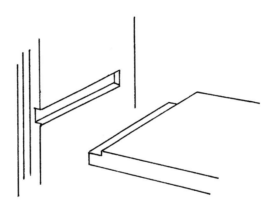

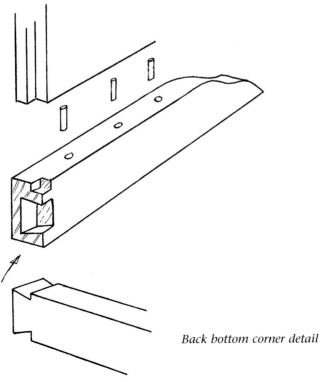

Back bottom corner detail

14 The top, which overhangs by ³/₄ in (19 mm) each side and to the front, is dowel jointed down into the top of each side upright and the two side plinths are also dowelled to the bottom of the side uprights. The bottom back rail is joined to the two side plinths by means of a single dovetail at each end. This provides a stable, upper frame and the joints resist any sideways pulling movement. Mark out and drill the top, the two plinths and the side uprights for dowelling. Cut the bottom back rail to length and mark out and cut the dovetail joints with which it is joined to the side plinths.

(15) Now have a dry assembly of all these components: side uprights, shelves, top, bottom back rail and plinths. Use webbing or another form of cramp to hold everything together if necessary. Check that all the pieces fit and check for squareness. While the components are assembled check the internal measurement for the top frieze. When this is made, and after shaping, it will be dowel jointed into position. Also, while the components are assembled, if a router is being used, the rebate which accommodates the back may be cut in one go; otherwise, if it is to be made by hand, each part, side, top and bottom rails, is done separately. The rebate is $1/2 \times 1/2$ in (13×13 mm).

(16) Disassemble the upper section. Make the rebate for the back if not previously done – the rebate in the top and bottom rails must be stopped at each end. Mark out and drill the side uprights and front frieze for dowelling.

(17) Assemble everything again dry, including the front frieze; check for squareness. Measure up for the back and cut boards to the required size. Ideally these should be dry jointed, either rebated or tongue-and-groove, to disguise the effect of any shrinkage.

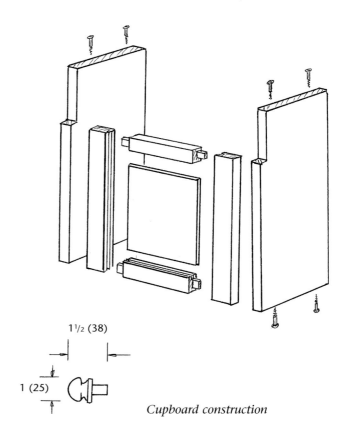

1½ (38)

1 (25)

Cupboard construction

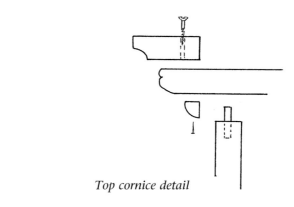

Top cornice detail

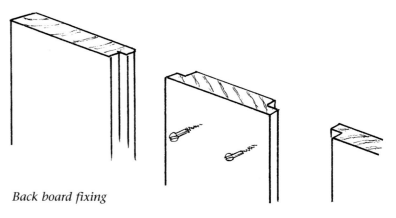

Back board fixing

(18) At this stage the side pieces for the spice cupboard – which can be regarded as something of an optional extra – can be measured up, cut and tried for fit. Notch them in behind the front frieze and screw them into place. Then disassemble everything again and drill the holes for the screws. Clean away all unwanted marks and prepare for gluing up.

(19) The sequence for gluing up is as follows. First fit the side plinths to the bottom end of the side uprights and, preferably, let these dry. Then fit first the front frieze between the two side uprights followed by the bottom rail, dovetailed into the side plinths. Next, put the spice cupboard sides into place and drop the top down on to all the dowels. Finally, slide the shelves in from the back and screw the spice cupboard sides into place. Cramp as required, remove any surplus glue, check for squareness and leave to dry and set.

(20) The back is now fitted into its prepared rebate where it is held in place by small screws (no. 4 × 1 in) or by panel pinning. The back boards will require pre-drilling before fitting to avoid splitting. The top moulding and beading are fitted, respectively, above and below the overhanging top to form a deep cornice. The corners are mitred and the pieces are glued and screwed or pinned into place as appropriate.

(21) Finally the spice cupboard door can be made. Take measurements from the opening in your cupboard and use those given only as a guide. Follow the instructions on page 60 to construct the door. Make it generous and trim to a neat fit. Hang on brass hinges and fit a small turned knob.

(22) The finish chosen for this piece of furniture will depend to some extent on its intended environment. A wax-polish finish is ideal for a living or dining room, but for a kitchen or scullery area a more robust finish such as Danish oil is recommended. See page 39 for advice on finishing.

Detail showing moulded cornice and shaped side member and frieze

Rocking Chair

More than any other item of furniture a rocking

chair evokes the strongest feeling

of the past and epitomizes the comfort of

leisured country living. The old American adage,

'Sometimes I rocks and thinks

and sometimes I just rocks', adequately sums

up the romance of the rocker.

Introduction Rocking chairs are thought to have developed simultaneously on both sides of the Atlantic towards the end of the eighteenth century. They later became extremely popular in some American states where they were, apparently, medically recommended for afterdinner relaxation and in consequence became known as 'digestive chairs'. In Victorian England, however, it seems that they were frowned upon and regarded as 'socially unacceptable'.

This difference in attitude is perhaps reflected in the fact that while American and some European rocking chairs were designed and purposely constructed to rock, in Britain there appear to have been few chairs, if any, specifically made with this action. Instead, chairs of an existing type and normally stationary could have rockers fitted to them by order of the purchaser. Trade catalogues of the period offered to add rockers, on request, for the cost of 1 shilling (5p) extra. An examination of the stretcher arrangement of many early English rocking chairs confirms this as the add-on rockers unnecessarily duplicate the side members of the usual 'H' stretcher configuration. Any chair having rockers is much stronger with double cross stretchers, as used in the chair described here.

Construction Details The chair is based on a traditional combback design. Instead of having turned sticks or spindles in the back, it has flat strips of wood subtly bent to conform to the shape of the lumbar curve; this arrangement makes it a very comfortable chair. Made in elm and apple wood for a special fiftieth-birthday present, it incorporates both turning and hand shaping and, while it requires some careful angle drilling, the device shown and the method described on page 37 will simplify this procedure.

Cutting List *(Add waste)*

No.	Item	in	mm
1	Seat	$20 \times 18^1/2 \times 1^3/4$	$508 \times 470 \times 44$
4	Legs	$15^1/2 \times 1^7/8 \times 1^7/8$	$394 \times 47 \times 47$
1	Front stretcher	$19 \times 1^1/2 \times 1^1/2$	$483 \times 38 \times 38$
1	Back stretcher	$17^1/2 \times 1^1/2 \times 1^1/2$	$445 \times 38 \times 38$
2	Arm supports	$11 \times 1^3/4 \times 1^3/4$	$279 \times 44 \times 44$
2	Back uprights (from)	$26 \times 3 \times 1^1/2$	$660 \times 76 \times 38$
6	Back laths	$24^1/2 \times 1^1/8 \times 3/8$	$623 \times 28 \times 10$
2	Arms	$13 \times 2^1/2 \times 2$	$330 \times 64 \times 51$
1	Comb (from)	$21^1/2 \times 6 \times 2^1/4$	$546 \times 152 \times 57$
2	Rockers (from)	$30 \times 5 \times 1^1/2$	$762 \times 127 \times 38$

Material Elm (seat) and apple, ash or beech

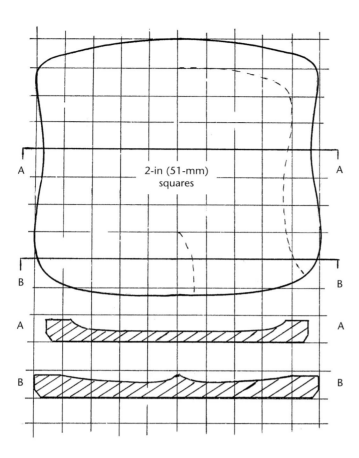

2-in (51-mm) squares

① Begin with the seat – the foundations of the chair. Use a single piece of wood if possible or grain match and edge joint separate, narrower pieces (see page 28 for jointing details). Cut the seat to the pattern given in the diagram and clean up the sawn edges. The broken line and profiles show the extent of hollowing (saddling) to be carried out later.

② Mark out the positions of the leg sockets on the underside of the seat and draw in the necessary alignment lines. Drill these holes at 1 in (25 mm) diameter and 1¹⁄₈ in (28 mm) deep and to the prescribed angles: back legs 20 degrees, front legs 10 degrees. Take particular care in starting to drill when working at a steep angle. The sloping platform device for angle drilling described on page 37 will prove helpful. The diagonal 'sight' lines are lined up on the centre line of the sloping platform to give consistent compound angles.

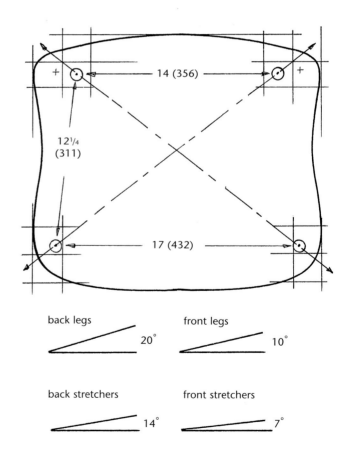

back legs 20°   front legs 10°

back stretchers 14°   front stretchers 7°

Drilled sockets in underside of seat

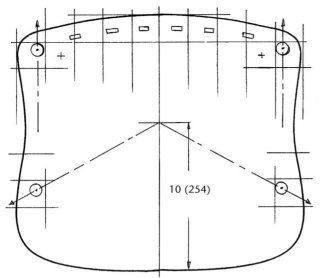

Drilled sockets in top of seat

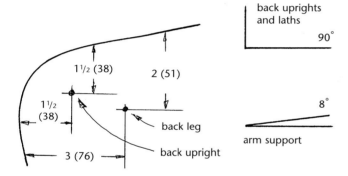

1½ (38)   2 (51)

1½ (38)

back uprights
and laths
90°

3 (76)   back leg
back upright

8°
arm support

Back corner detail

③ Mark out the top component positions to accommodate the back uprights, back laths and arm supports. Draw in the alignment line for the arm stumps. Drill the back upright sockets 1 in (25 mm) diameter and right through the seat: drill vertically (90 degrees). Drill the arm supports 1 in (25 mm) diameter and 1 in (25 mm) deep, at an outward angle of 8 degrees. The back lath sockets are vertical too and cut 5/16 in (8 mm) wide and to a depth of ¾ inch (19 mm) by careful drilling and chiselling – leave the end of the sockets rounded.

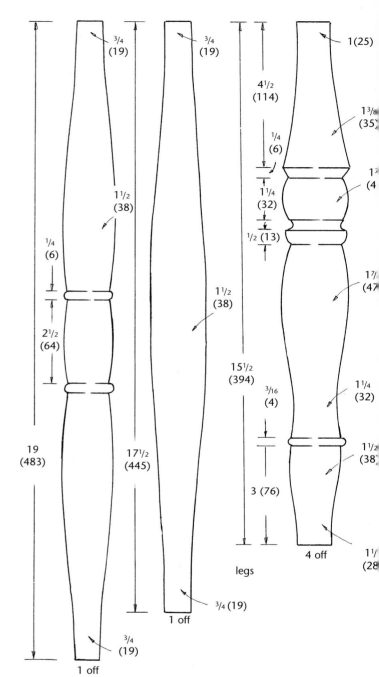

¾ (19)   ¾ (19)

1½ (38)

¼ (6)

2½ (64)

19 (483)

1½ (38)

17½ (445)

1 off   ¾ (19)

stretchers

1 off   ¾ (19)

1 off

1(25)

4½ (114)

1³/₈ (35)

¼ (6)

1¼ (32)

1½ (13)

1

1½ (38)

1¼ (32)

15½ (394)

³/₁₆ (4)

3 (76)

4 off

legs

④ Mark out the area of the seat to be hollowed (saddled) according to the pattern and rough out to the drawn line and profiles shown on page 86. Do this using any safe means available. Leave the final finish until later.

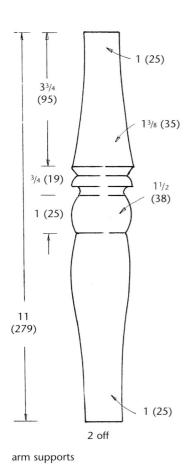

1 (25)

3³/₄ (95)

1³/₈ (35)

³/₄ (19)

1 (25)

1¹/₂ (38)

11 (279)

1 (25)

2 off

arm supports

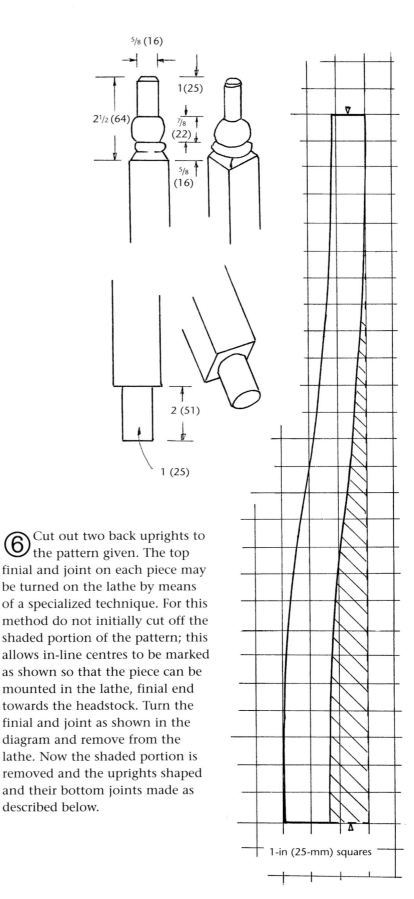

⁵/₈ (16)

2¹/₂ (64)

1 (25)

7/8 (22)

⁵/₈ (16)

2 (51)

1 (25)

1-in (25-mm) squares

⑤ Now make all the turned components: four legs, two stretchers and two arm supports. Work to the patterns given, or choose your own design, but retain the overall length and joint dimensions as given. The stretchers are generous in length and will require some final adjustment at a trial assembly later.

⑥ Cut out two back uprights to the pattern given. The top finial and joint on each piece may be turned on the lathe by means of a specialized technique. For this method do not initially cut off the shaded portion of the pattern; this allows in-line centres to be marked as shown so that the piece can be mounted in the lathe, finial end towards the headstock. Turn the finial and joint as shown in the diagram and remove from the lathe. Now the shaded portion is removed and the uprights shaped and their bottom joints made as described below.

⑦ Alternatively, the finials and top and bottom joints may be cut and shaped by hand. In this case the uprights are cut out completely and then, from just above the arm joint area, tapered to 1¼ in (32 mm) at the top. Mark out the finial and top joint as shown and square the lines all around. Saw cut carefully on these lines and chisel, gouge or knife cut to shape. Keep the tenon round and to full size; test fit in a 5/8-in- (16-mm)-diameter hole. Round over the edges of the upright but only from above the arm joint area. Mark out and shape the bottom joint tenon in a similar way – it must be long enough to go well through the seat thickness. Test fit in the socket already drilled in the seat.

⑧ The arms are cut out to the pattern given; make a left and then make a right by reversing the pattern, trying to match the arms' grain and figure. The arms attach to the back uprights in a shallow housing and are retained by means of a concealed screw: this is a relatively simple joint to make if care is taken with the marking out. Care must also be taken with drilling the sockets for the arm supports in the underside of the arms. Mark the position of each socket and drill inward at an angle of 8 degrees, 1 in (25 mm) diameter and 1 in (25 mm) deep. Do all this in the following sequence.

⑨ First drill the underside of the arm as described in stage 8. Fit the arm support in the socket in the seat; fit the back upright into position. Then fit the arm fully on to the arm support and lie the arm alongside the back upright. Mark the position of the arm on the back upright. It should be as shown in the diagram, but it is best to check this. Trim the arm length, if necessary: it should be housed no more than ¼ in (6 mm) into the back upright. Cut the housing and test fit the arm. While it is in position, mark out for the screw clearance and counter-bored hole in the back upright. Remove the back upright and drill. Test fit everything again until satisfactory.

Back view of the rocking chair, clearly showing the curve of the back laths to suit the curve of the sitter's back

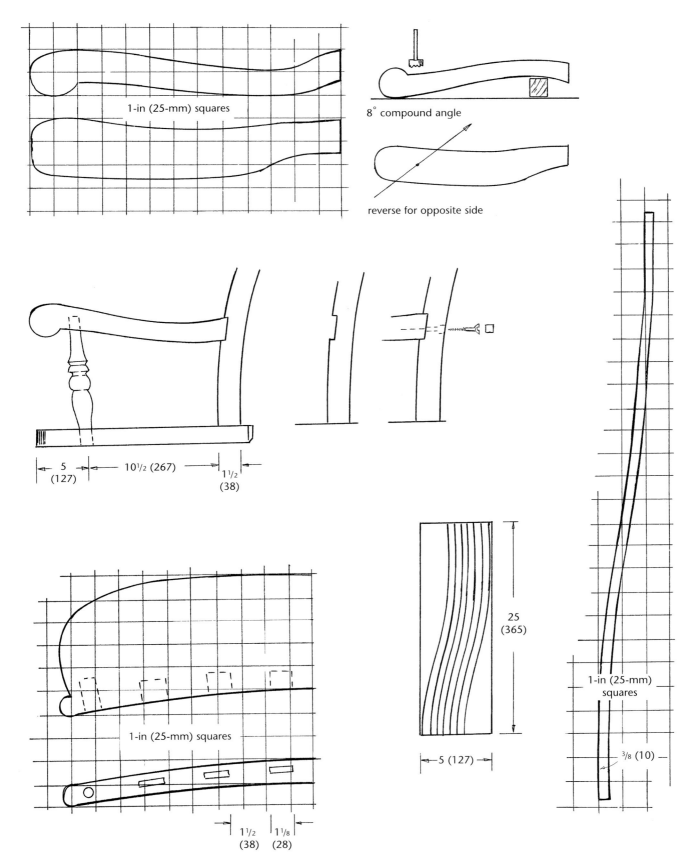

1-in (25-mm) squares

8° compound angle

reverse for opposite side

5 (127)   10½ (267)   1½ (38)

25 (365)

5 (127)

1-in (25-mm) squares

1-in (25-mm) squares

1½ (38)   1⅛ (28)

3/8 (10)

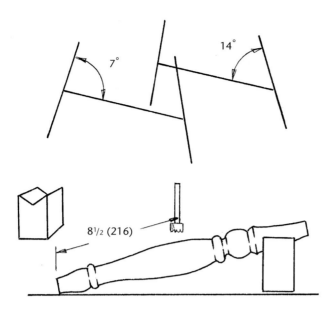

14°

7°

8½ (216)

Drilling sockets for stretchers

10 The curved shape of the comb is cut out and the broad surfaces smoothed. Do not shape the top edge until after the bottom edge is drilled and slotted for the back components. Mark out and drill the back upright sockets, 5/8 in (16 mm) diameter and 1 in (25 mm) deep, and make the back lath sockets, 5/16 in (8 mm) wide and 3/4 in (19 mm) deep, by careful drilling and chiselling – leave the ends of these sockets rounded. Cut and smooth the comb to its finished shape.

11 Cut out the six curved back laths economically as shown in the diagram on page 91 and, after you have cleaned them up, fit them individually first into their respective sockets in the seat, then into the comb. The 3/8-in (10-mm) laths will require trimming to give a neat, gap-free fit in the 5/16-in (8-mm) sockets cut for them.

12 Now with all components, except the rockers, made, have a trial assembly, without glue. Begin with the underframe and seat; place the seat on a flat, protected surface and test fit the legs individually, orientating the grain figure to best advantage. Mark the position of the cross stretchers on each leg, remove and drill the stretcher sockets: front 7 degrees, back 14 degrees; 3/4 in (19 mm) diameter, 3/4 in (19 mm) deep. Replace the legs in their correct sockets and check the stretcher lengths; adjust if necessary – remember that stretchers should stretch legs apart and should not be made too short. Everything should be under slight tension. Check for stability on a level surface; adjust if necessary.

13 Then test fit, without glue, the top components. Fit and screw the arms to the back uprights and put the arm supports in place in the seat. Fit the back uprights, bringing the arms down on to the uprising arm supports. You will find that the round tenon of the back uprights into the seat provides a rotary movement, allowing the arms to be positioned correctly. Fit the back laths into their respective sockets, then lower the comb into position on the back upright tenons and manipulate each back lath into its comb socket. Tap the comb down gently and check that it lies correctly. All should go together under slight tension.

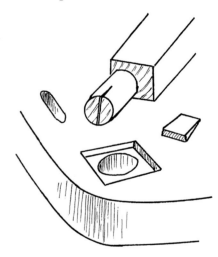

Back upright joint detail

14 To improve the back upright bottom joint, recess it slightly into the surface of the seat. While the top components are assembled, carefully mark around the end of each back upright in contact with the seat surface with a sharp pointed knife to delineate this recess. Disassemble all the top components.

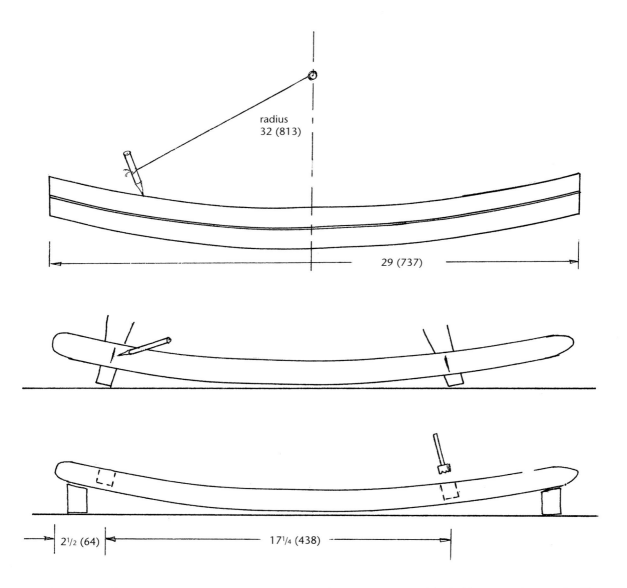

radius
32 (813)

29 (737)

2¹/₂ (64) 17¹/₄ (438)

Marking out rockers

⑮ With the underframe still assembled, the rockers can now be marked out for fitting. Mark out the two rockers to the given radius of 32 in (813 mm) by using a piece of string of that length tied to a pencil and held central to the arc. Saw the rockers to shape. Then, with the seat and underframe standing on a level surface, place each rocker alongside the legs and mark the position for the leg sockets. Mark 'slight' lines as shown. Drill sockets 1 in (25 mm) diameter and 1 in (25 mm) deep, supporting each rocker on a small wedge to give the necessary compound angle. Drill down in line with the marked 'slight' lines. Test fit on the legs; mark left and right. Remove the rockers and clean up, rounding over all the sharp edges. Disassemble the remainder of the underframe.

16 Now carefully cut out the previously marked recesses for the back uprights into the seat surface; these should be 3/16 in (4 mm) deep. Test fit the uprights to obtain a neat, gap-free fit. When this is satisfactory, mark the ends of the round tenons for saw cuts to accommodate wedges from underneath which tighten the joint. The saw cuts must run across the grain of the seat to prevent the seat being split when the wedges are driven in. Saw the two cuts and make the wedges.

17 Complete the seat shaping: smooth over the saddled area, ensuring that the front top edge is smoothly rounded for comfort; work a substantial chamfer on the bottom edge and a smaller one on the top edge. Clean all the other components, removing any unwanted marks, and prepare for gluing up.

18 Begin by gluing up the underframe and seat. With the seat upside down on a flat, protected surface, put glue into the leg sockets in the seat and into the stretcher sockets in the legs. Fit the legs part-way into their respective sockets, add the stretchers and push or tap everything into place. Check that all joints go to full depth. Check on a level surface for stability. Do not fit the rockers until later.

19 Now add the top components. Glue and screw together the arms and back uprights. Put glue into the arm supports' sockets and into the back uprights' sockets, into the recesses in the seat and into the underarm sockets. Put the arm supports in place and orientate for the best grain figure; fit the back uprights with the arms in place by bringing down each upright and arm unit on to the uprising arm support and guiding the back uprights into the seat recesses. Press or tap everything into position. Fit wedges in the back upright tenons underneath and hammer in tight. Clean off flush later. Put glue in the back lath sockets and partly fit the laths. Put glue into all the sockets in the under edge of the comb and bring this down on to the uprising back laths and back upright top tenons. Tap down and check that the comb lies correctly. Finally fit the rockers; put glue into each of the sockets and enter the legs to full depth. Clean off any surplus glue and leave to dry.

20 The best finish for a chair of this type is sanding sealer followed by a good-quality wax polish. See page 39 for finishing details.

Credence Cupboard

Ecclesiastic by association, this precious piece typifies the simple but sound furniture made during the late sixteenth century and later – the Age of Oak – and used in the churches and manor houses of the period. The methods of the medieval craftsman are clearly to be seen in its manner of construction.

Introduction Based on an early English design, this type of cupboard was used during the sixteenth century, and later, for the storage of food. The openings in the doors, with their row of turned spindles, are clearly for ventilation purposes. Often used to dispense or deliver the rations of food and drink to servants, they became known as livery cupboards, from the French *livrer*, meaning to deliver. In churches they were similarly used for the storage or distribution of dole – alms in the form of basic food for the poor and needy; consequently these were called dole cupboards. It was their alternative use not only for storing but also for serving bread and wine during the act of Holy Communion that gave rise to the name credence cupboard.

Construction Details In keeping with its historical context, this cupboard was made in English oak and constructed in a largely traditional way. The mortise-and-tenon joints were glued but also secured and pulled tight by the medieval draw bore method described on page 35. This method, used long before glue, ensures that tenon shoulders pull up tight and it also eliminates the need for long cramps at assembly. Hand-made, wrought-iron hinges were used to hang the doors, fixed with iron nails, clenched over for security. Simple, decorative features such as edge beading and chamfering were hand done. The completed cupboard was lightly distressed and stained and polished to the client's requirements by my friend and colleague Adrian Errey.

Cutting List *(Add waste)*

No.	Item	in	mm
4	Corner posts	32 × 2¹/2 × 1¹/2	813 × 64 × 38
2	Front rails	37¹/2 × 2¹/2 × 1¹/8	953 × 64 × 28
2	Back rails	37¹/2 × 2¹/2 × 1¹/8	953 × 64 × 28
4	Side rails	20 × 2¹/2 × 1¹/8	508 × 64 × 28
1	Top (to make)	42 × 21 × 1	1067 × 533 × 25
1	Bottom (to make)	37 × 21 × ¹/2	940 × 533 × 13
2	Side panels (to make)	21 × 18¹/2 × ¹/2	533 × 470 × 13
1	Back panel (to make)	37 × 21 × ³/8	940 × 533 × 10
4	Door stiles	20 × 2 × 1¹/8	508 × 51 × 28
6	Door rails	16 × 2 × 1¹/8	406 × 51 × 28
2	Panels	14¹/2 × 10 × ³/8	369 × 254 × 10
10	Turned spindles	5 × ⁷/8 × ⁷/8	127 × 22 × 22
2	Battens	34 × ³/4 × ³/4	864 × 19 × 19
2	Battens	17¹/2 × ³/4 × ³/4	445 × 19 × 19

Material Oak.

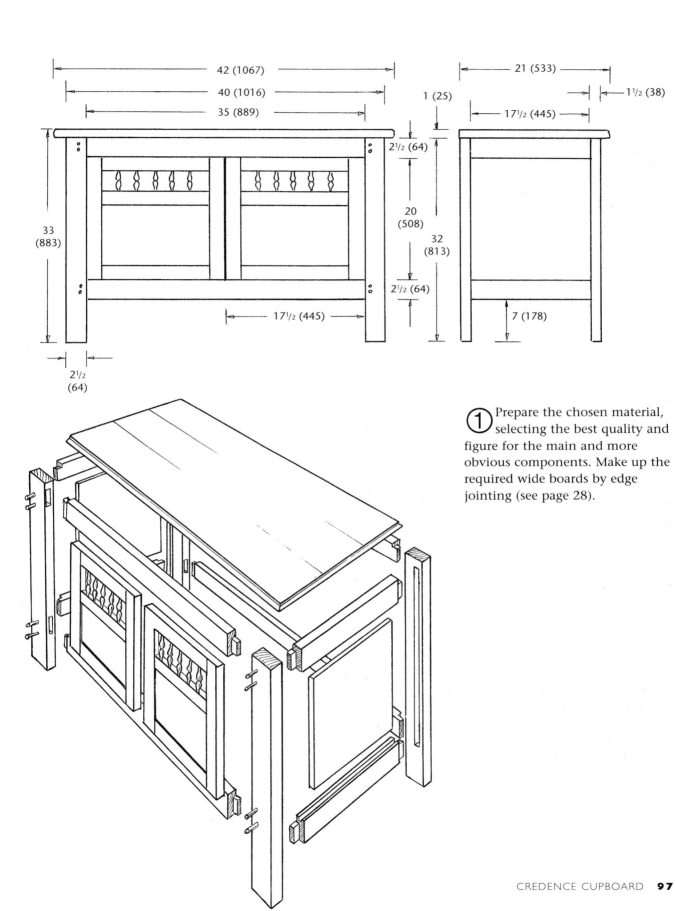

42 (1067)

40 (1016)

35 (889)

1 (25)

2¹/₂ (64)

33 (883)

20 (508)

32 (813)

2¹/₂ (64)

17¹/₂ (445)

2¹/₂ (64)

21 (533)

1¹/₂ (38)

17¹/₂ (445)

7 (178)

① Prepare the chosen material, selecting the best quality and figure for the main and more obvious components. Make up the required wide boards by edge jointing (see page 28).

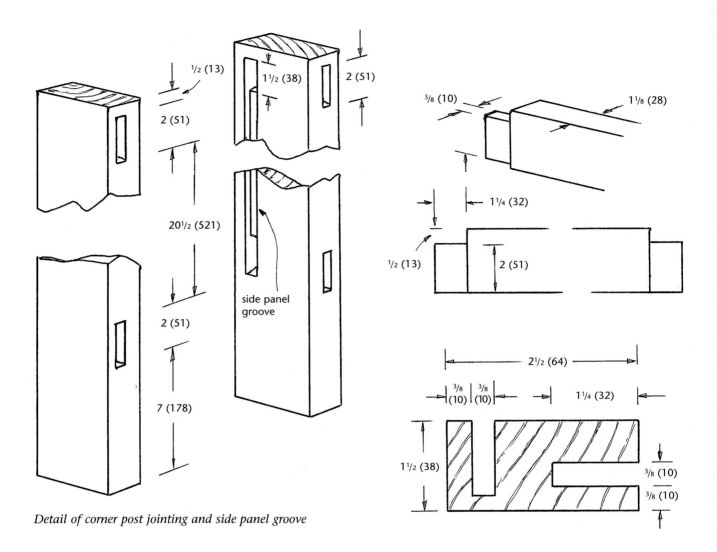

Detail of corner post jointing and side panel groove

2 Begin with the four corner posts. Mark out, all together to ensure conformity, for the four mortises in each and cut these to a depth of 1¼ in (32 mm). Note that the side rail mortises are smaller than those for the front and back rails. See page 100.

3 Then cut the stopped groove in each post which accommodates the side panels. (If using a router to make these grooves, keep it at the same setting for use at stage 6.) See the diagram on page 100.

4 Next, accurately measure the shoulder length of the two front rails and the two back rails and mark out and cut the required tenons (see page 32). Try these individually for a good fit in their respective mortises, which are those on the narrow edge of the corner posts.

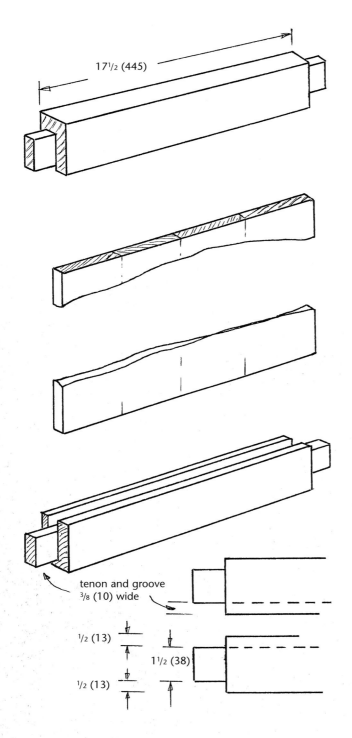

17½ (445)

tenon and groove
³⁄₈ (10) wide

½ (13)

1½ (38)

½ (13)

Side frame and panel

⑤ Now have a dry assembly – without glue – of these front and back frame sections and check for fit and squareness. While they are assembled, prepare all the joints for draw pegging (see page 35). Mark all the joints for ease of identification at the assembly stage and then disassemble.

⑥ Measure the shoulder length of the four side rails and mark out and cut the tenons on these. Note that they are smaller than the ones on the front and back rails to take account of the side panel groove. Cut the groove on the inner edge of each rail. (Some workers cut the panel grooves before mortising. This has it advantages, but it is largely a matter of personal choice.)

⑦ Try each tenon individually in its respective mortise and when they are satisfactory have a dry assembly of the corner posts and end rails. Check for fit and squareness. While they are assembled, measure the required size of the side panels. (The measurements shown are given as a guide only.) Disassemble.

⑧ Cut the two end panels to size and square and trim their edges to be a loose fit in the panel grooves.

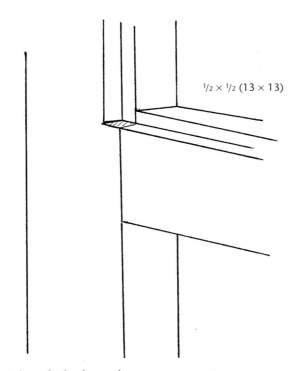

1/2 × 1/2 (13 × 13)

Rebate for back panel

11 This is also a good time to work the decorative stopped chamfer on the outside edges of each of the four corner posts. Do this by hand with a sharp chisel and a small plane or spokeshave.

12 Clean off all unwanted marks and smooth all surfaces as required, then glue up. Begin by making up the side sections, putting the side panels in without glue – they must be free to allow for movement. Cramp up and check for squareness; clean off any surplus glue and leave to dry.

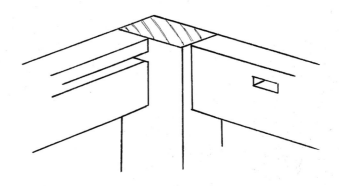

9 Now assemble, dry, the complete cupboard frame and end panels. Do this with the cupboard standing on a level surface. Check the diagonals and check the door opening for squareness. While these pieces are assembled, mark the position and extent of the rebate to house the back. Then disassemble and cut the 1/2-in (13-mm) rebate for the back.

10 The top, when fitted, is held in place by means of 'buttons', as shown in the diagram, which allow for any movement of the wood that may occur. The slots which accommodate these buttons may be cut into the inside edge of the top front and back and the top side rails now with ease rather than later with difficulty.

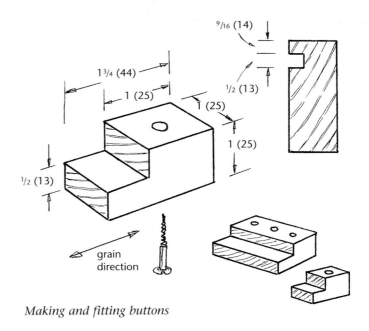

9/16 (14)

1 3/4 (44)

1 (25)

1 (25)

1/2 (13)

1/2 (13)

1 (25)

grain direction

Making and fitting buttons

Detail of the credence cupboard, showing the turned spindles and the hand-made, wrought-iron hinges

⑬ When the side sections are dry and set, add the front and back rails and drive in the pegs which secure the front and back mortise-and-tenon joints. Stand the piece on a level surface and check that the carcass and in particular the door opening are square. Clean off any surplus glue and leave to dry and set.

⑭ Before proceeding further it is advisable to check the measurements for the cupboard bottom, back and top, and also the precise size of the door opening. These dimensions are given, but it is best to check against your own work.

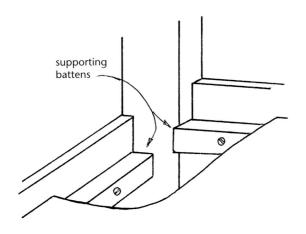

supporting
battens

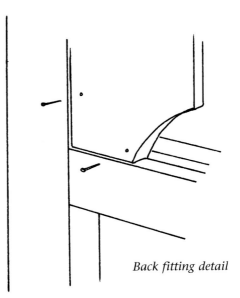

Bottom fitting detail

Back fitting detail

⑮ Cut to size and fit the bottom. It is supported on battens which are screwed and glued to the bottom rails as shown. The bottom may be screwed or pegged into place on these battens.

⑯ Cut to size and fit the back. It should be a snug fit in the back rebate where it is screwed or nailed into place. Pre-drill to avoid splitting.

⑰ Now make the doors. Be generous and make two slightly oversize doors which can be trimmed to fit. Begin by cutting the four uprights or stiles to length, then the six rails. Make the grooves which accommodate the door panels: $3/8$ in (10 mm) wide, and $3/8$ in (10 mm) deep. Note the extent of this groove on the stiles.(See page 104.)

⑱ Mark out and cut the mortises – three in each stile – the same width as the groove and $1^1/4$ in (32 mm) deep.

Detail showing the hand-carved date on the front rail of the cupboard. Note the draw bore pegs

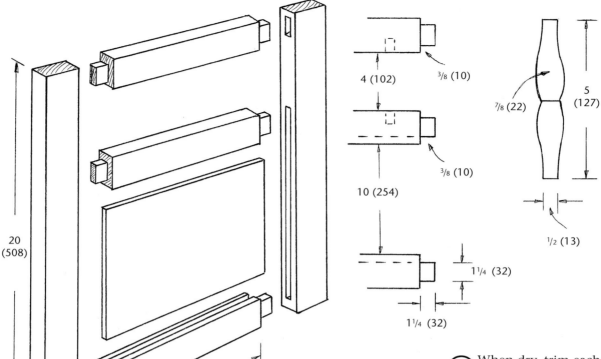

4 (102)

³⁄₈ (10)

³⁄₈ (10)

10 (254)

1¹⁄₄ (32)

1¹⁄₄ (32)

5 (127)

⁷⁄₈ (22)

¹⁄₂ (13)

20 (508)

13¹⁄₂ (343)

⑲ Measure the required shoulder length of the door rail tenons and mark out and cut the rail tenons. Note their diversity.

⑳ Try each joint individually, trimming to a good fit as necessary. When satisfied, assemble the door frames without glue and check for squareness. Check the measurements for the door panels. Prepare the corner joints for draw pegging (see page 35). Disassemble.

㉑ Cut the door panels to size; reduce their edges to fit correctly in the grooves already made. This process, known as fielding, can be done by careful planing.

㉒ The ventilation slot in each door has a row of simple, turned spindles and these must be made and fitted before the doors are finally glued up and assembled. The spindles are fitted into holes drilled as shown in the diagram. Have a dry assembly to check that everything fits together, then disassemble.

㉓ Clean off unwanted marks, smooth all surfaces as required and glue up. With the turned spindles already in position, add the door panels, without glue, and make up each door. Drive the pegs into the corner joints. Check for squareness, remove any surplus glue and leave to dry and set.

㉔ When dry, trim each door to a good fit in the opening. Hang the doors on good-quality butt hinges or, as in this case, on wrought-iron hinges. Fit a suitable door catch.

㉕ Check that the top is cut to size to give a 1-in (25-mm) overlap all round. Round over the front and side edges and work a simple, beaded mould all around. Make and fit the 'buttons' – see the diagram on page 101 (below right) – and fit the top to the cupboard.

㉖ Apply a finish of your choice. This example was lightly distressed, stained and polished professionally in accordance with the client's request to 'make it look old'. See page 39 for advice on simple finishing methods. (The cupboard had a date carved on the top front rail in Roman numerals in keeping with its period appearance: MCMXCVII or 1997!)

Kitchen Chair

This charming piece is typical of rural chairs
the world over – all across Europe and
parts of Asia and, through settlement, in the
Americas and Australasia too. Its simple construction
and hand-woven seat place it firmly in the realm
of peasant craft and, plain or painted,
it looks well in any situation.

Introduction This is an interpretation of a simple cottage chair in common use throughout the nineteenth and early twentieth centuries. These chairs, like so many other early domestic chairs of the type, were smaller in size than the one described here. According to one school of thought, chairs used to be smaller because people were, but a more plausible explanation is linked to the way in which family life centred around the hearth, the fireplace being the principal source of both heat and light; it was where people cooked, ate, talked and made music. Because the fire was low down on the floor, seating was correspondingly low to obtain best advantage from it. Low seating may also have made it easier to keep heads beneath the pall of smoke often present in the usually chimneyless dwellings. When, later, the table replaced the hearth as the domestic gathering place, chair heights and overall size were increased to those more common today to make sitting at the table more comfortable.

Construction Details An important attribute of these chairs, described in the USA as being of post-and-rail construction, is their sturdy simplicity. With the exception of the two upper back rails, all constructional joints consist of easily formed, round tenons on round rails jointed into round sockets in rectangular uprights (posts). The two upper back rails are slot mortised full width into the back uprights. These are shaped to a slight curve for comfort. To provide both an angled back for further comfort and a sufficient backward rake to the leg portion to give adequate stability, the back uprights are also curved; for reasons of economy the back uprights are sawn 'back to back' from a single piece of timber. On completion the seat is woven using either plaited rush or ready-twisted sea-grass cord.

Cutting List *(Add waste)*			
No.	*Item*	*in*	*mm*
2	Back uprights (from)	$36 \times 6 \times 1^3/_8$	$914 \times 152 \times 35$
2	Front legs	$18 \times 1^7/_8 \times 1^3/_8$	$457 \times 47 \times 35$
2	Upper back rails	$17 \times 3 \times 2^1/_2$	$432 \times 76 \times 64$
1	Front seat rail	$17 \times 1 \times 1$	$432 \times 25 \times 25$
1	Front stretcher	$17 \times 1 \times 1$	$432 \times 25 \times 25$
1	Back seat rail	$15 \times 1 \times 1$	$381 \times 25 \times 25$
2	Side seat rails	$15 \times 1 \times 1$	$381 \times 25 \times 25$
2	Upper side stretchers	$15^3/_4 \times 1 \times 1$	$400 \times 25 \times 25$
2	Lower side stretchers	$16^1/_2 \times 1 \times 1$	$419 \times 25 \times 25$
1	Back stretcher	$15 \times 1 \times 1$	$381 \times 25 \times 25$

Material Ash or beech.

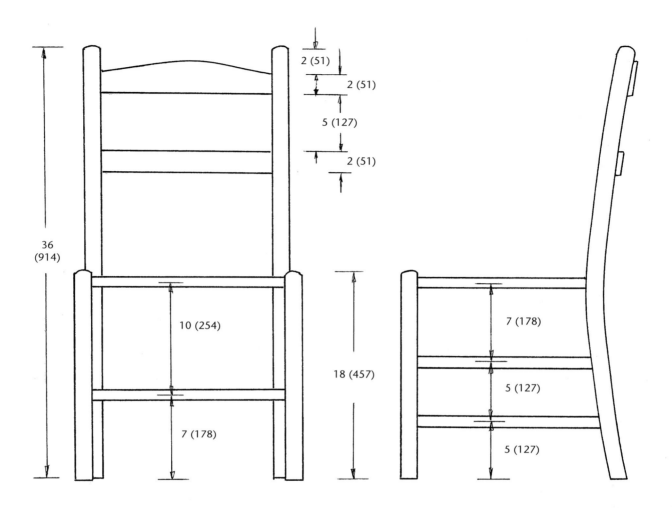

2 (51)

2 (51)

5 (127)

2 (51)

36
(914)

10 (254)

7 (178)

18 (457)

7 (178)

5 (127)

5 (127)

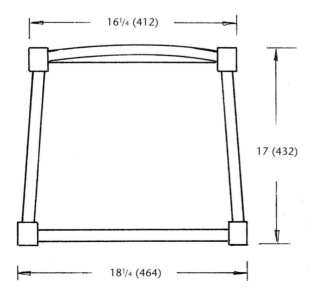

16¼ (412)

17 (432)

18¼ (464)

① Select sound, straight-grained material, especially for the small-diameter round components, to ensure maximum strength.

② Begin by planing flat and smooth what will be the side surfaces of the two back uprights. Then mark out their slightly curving shape and saw or bandsaw these according to the pattern on page 109. Check their length carefully.

③ Clean up the sawn edges and round over their top ends. Final smoothing can be left until later.

④ Plane flat and smooth the two front legs, tapering them as shown in the pattern. Round over their top ends; leave sufficient square at this point to retain the seat weaving material which will be applied later.

⑤ Turn or otherwise make round the four seat rails and the seven stretcher rails. Because the chair is wider at the front than at the back, and because of the backward 'splay' of the back legs, these vary in length. Check their respective lengths carefully according to their location in the chair, and also see below.

⑥ The back and side seat rails are the same length, 15 in (381 mm), while the front seat rail is 2 in (51 mm) longer at 17 in (432 mm). The seat rails need not be made smooth; they will be covered and concealed by the woven seat.

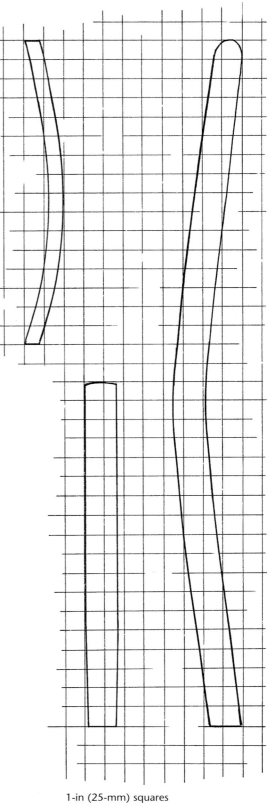

1-in (25-mm) squares

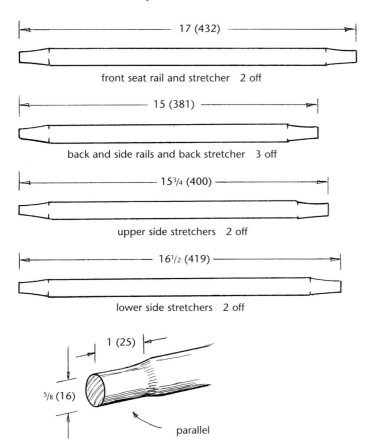

17 (432)

front seat rail and stretcher   2 off

15 (381)

back and side rails and back stretcher   3 off

15³/₄ (400)

upper side stretchers   2 off

16¹/₂ (419)

lower side stretchers   2 off

1 (25)

⁵/₈ (16)

parallel

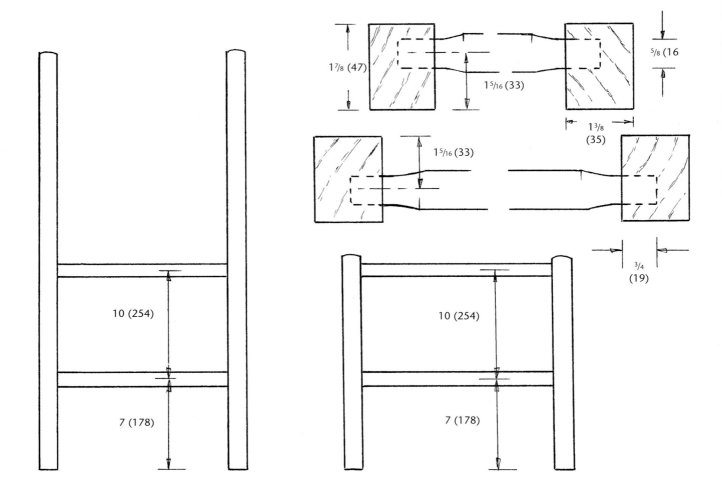

Back and front 'ladders'

⑦ The back stretcher is also 15 in (381 mm) long but, to accommodate the backward splay of the back legs, the two upper side stretchers (left and right) are 3/4 in (19 mm) longer at 15 3/4 in (400 mm) and their lower counterparts are longer again by 3/4 in (19 mm) at 16 1/2 in (419 mm). The front stretcher is 17 in (432 mm) in length.

⑧ All seat rails and stretchers are 1 in (25 mm) in diameter, their ends reduced to 5/8 in (16 mm) diameter to form round tenon joints. These joint areas must be accurate in size if tight joints are to be achieved.

⑨ Finally mark out the two slightly curving upper back rails and saw or bandsaw according to the pattern on page 109. Clean up the sawn surfaces: leave the pieces generous in length at this stage.

⑩ Now, with all the component parts made, work can begin on marking out the vertical members – front and back legs – for drilling the round sockets for the seat rails and stretchers. This is best done in strict sequence, regarding the chair as a back 'ladder' and a front 'ladder' which are then joined together by the side rails.

11 First mark out the position of the back seat rail and stretchers on the 'inside' surfaces of the two back uprights. Note that these are 'off centre' – see the diagram on page 110 (above right). Drill at the marked positions, 5/8 in (16 mm) diameter, 3/4 in (19 mm) deep and vertical.

12 Then mark out the position of the front seat rail and stretchers on the inside surfaces of the two front legs. These too are drilled 'off centre'. Drill at the marked positions, 5/8 in (16 mm) diameter, 3/4 in (19 mm) deep and vertical.

13 Check that the individual rails and stretchers fit their respective sockets and go to full depth, then have a first dry assembly – without glue – joining pairs of vertical members to make a back 'ladder' and a front 'ladder'. Place on a flat surface and check for wind; adjust by gently twisting if necessary.

14 With back and front 'ladders' still assembled, mark out, on a centre line, the position of the side seat and side stretcher rails on both assemblies. Because the chair is wider at the front than at the back, these sockets will be drilled at an angle, at 5 degrees greater than 90 degrees for the back legs, 5 degrees less than 90 degrees for the front legs. In effect, side rails into back uprights angle outwards, side rails into front legs angle inwards. See the diagram below for details.

15 Disassemble and drill all these sockets at 5/8 in (16 mm) diameter, 3/4 in (19 mm) deep. Follow the angle drilling method described on page 37.

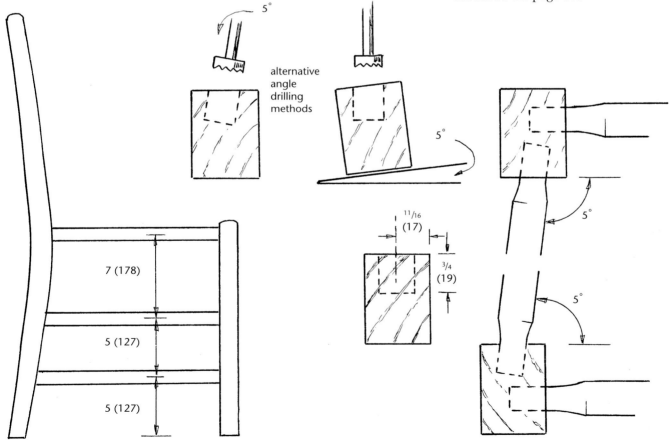

5°

alternative angle drilling methods

5°

7 (178)

5 (127)

5 (127)

11/16 (17)

3/4 (19)

5°

5°

Side rails and stretchers

Drilling angles

16 After checking that individual side rails and stretchers fit their respective sockets and go to full depth, assemble the back and front 'ladders' again without glue. Then add the side rails and stretchers in their correct positions to complete the main chair frame. Ensure that all joints go to full depth. Stand on a level surface and check for stability.

17 With the chair frame assembled, you can ascertain the correct length of the two curved upper back rails. Shorten the rails if necessary.

18 Disassemble, identifying the components for ease of assembly later. Then mark the position of the slot mortises for the upper back rails on the inside surfaces of the two back uprights as shown. Note that these mortises are marked in line with the back seat rail and stretchers and are cut at a backward angle to allow for the curvature of the upper back rails.

19 Cut these mortises by drilling and careful chiselling. Shape the upper back rails as shown and reduce the thickness of their ends to be a tight, neat fit in their respective mortises. As a further check, have a dry assembly of the complete back 'ladder' components and then of the complete chair.

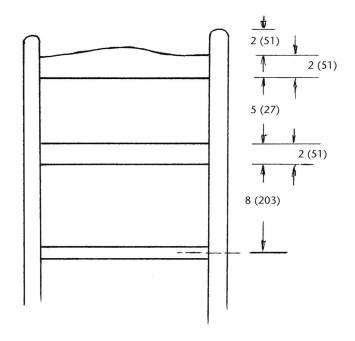

2 (51)

2 (51)

5 (27)

2 (51)

8 (203)

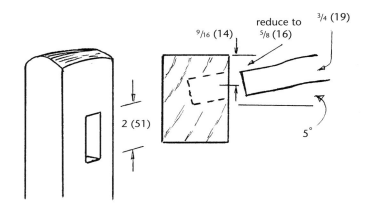

9/16 (14)

reduce to 5/8 (16)

3/4 (19)

2 (51)

5°

Upper back rails: jointing details

20 When everything is satisfactory, disassemble, clean and smooth all components and prepare for gluing up.

21 Begin final gluing up by assembling the complete front and back 'ladders', checking these on a level surface for wind. Then add the side seat rails and stretchers. Ensure that all joints go to full depth. Stand the chair frame on a level surface and check for stability. If the joints are tight, cramping should not be necessary, but may be used if required. Wipe off any surplus glue and leave to dry.

22 A suitable finish for kitchen use would be an oil such as Danish oil. Alternatively use sanding sealer and wax. See page 39 for finishing details.

23 The seat would traditionally have been woven with rush (*Scirpus lacustris*), an aquatic plant. Today this material is quite expensive and it is difficult to weave well without practice. An easier, and less expensive, alternative is to use imported sea grass, a ready-twisted, natural cord (see the diagram).

24 Rush must be made 'mellow' and pliable by soaking in water. Two or more strands are twisted together as the work proceeds and joined on as required. Sea-grass cord comes in long coils (or hanks) and is ready-twisted. For square or rectangular seats follow the sequence shown in A, B and C. For seats wider at the front (as in this case) first fill the extra length of the front rail (D), then follow the normal sequence (E).

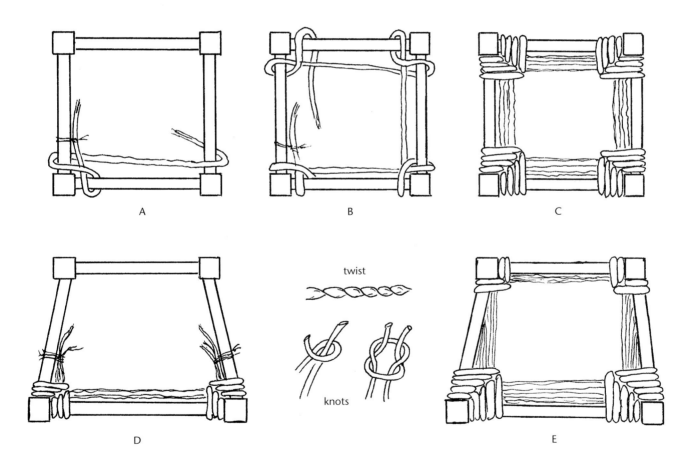

Seat weaving sequence

Joyned Stool

This desirable little stool takes its name

from the medieval spelling of joiner, which

has survived from the days when trade guilds strictly

regulated the work of individual craftsmen.

It is an excellent example of the combined efforts

of woodturner and joiner and

a joy to make.

Introduction Until about the middle of the seventeenth century there were few chairs and these were always reserved for persons of status: hence the term 'chairman', more recently updated to 'chair person'. Lesser beings sat on benches or stools. The earliest stools were slabs of wood with feet socketed in them. Later stools were of the trestle type (small versions of the table, page 123) and these in turn were replaced by the framed-up, jointed or joyned stool. Sturdily made with its board seat on a framework of top rails and stretchers mortised and tenoned into robust, turned legs, the joyned stool was a common article of domestic furniture until well into the eighteenth century.

This type of stool should not be confused with the much lower foot stools of the period; it was intended to serve as seating at a table and its seat height was therefore similar to that of early chairs. Sets of six or more were apparently fairly common at one time. Today pairs of joyned stools are sometimes referred to as 'coffin stools'; but supporting the dead was never their prime purpose.

Many of these stools were decorated with carving and some had elaborate, bulbous legs. The stool described here is of the more simple, country variety with plain sides and column or 'gun-barrel' legs.

Construction Details Made true to the recognized seventeenth-century style, the stool described here was built in oak and has legs which splay or are angled outwards to the sides. The joint used in its construction is the bare-faced mortise-and-tenon, and to accommodate the splayed legs the joints on the ends have tenons with sloping or canted shoulders. These are marked out with a sliding bevel set to the required angle instead of the more usual try square. Corresponding angled mortises are cut into the legs to match this same angle. Completed joints are tightened and secured by the draw bore method of pegging (see page 35). The legs are lathe turned with portions left square for jointing purposes.

Cutting List (Add waste)			
No.	Item	in	mm
4	Legs	$15^{1}/_{2} \times 1^{3}/_{4} \times 1^{3}/_{4}$	$394 \times 44 \times 44$
2	Top side rails	$13^{3}/_{4} \times 3 \times {}^{7}/_{8}$	$349 \times 76 \times 22$
2	Top end rails	$7^{3}/_{4} \times 3 \times {}^{7}/_{8}$	$197 \times 76 \times 22$
2	Bottom side rails	$13^{3}/_{4} \times 1^{1}/_{2} \times {}^{7}/_{8}$	$349 \times 38 \times 22$
2	Bottom end rails	$9^{1}/_{4} \times 1^{1}/_{2} \times {}^{7}/_{8}$	$235 \times 38 \times 22$
1	Top (to make)	$18 \times 12 \times {}^{1}/_{2}$	$457 \times 305 \times 13$

Material Oak.

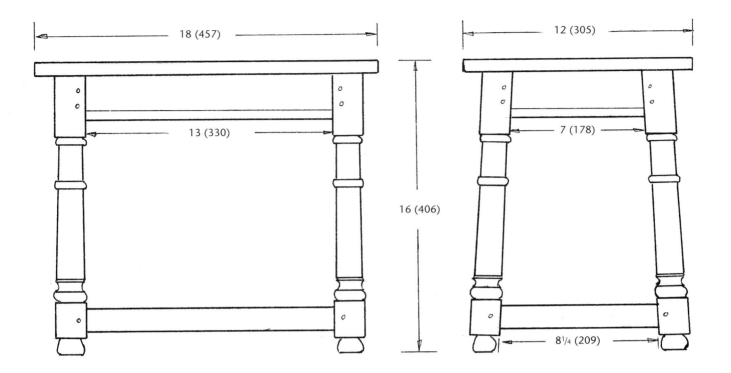

18 (457)

12 (305)

13 (330)

7 (178)

16 (406)

8¼ (209)

① Begin by selecting good-quality material and plane everything square and true to the dimensions given.

② Make up the top or seat piece by edge jointing two narrower boards. Glue up and cramp and leave to set and dry. (See page 28 for edge jointing details.)

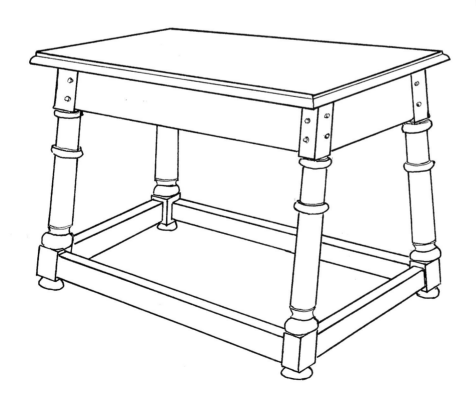

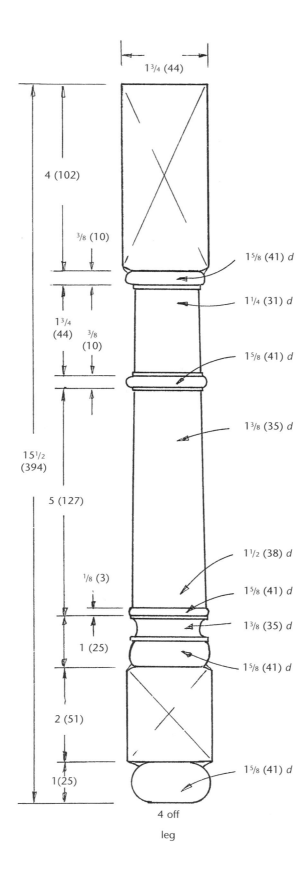

1³/₄ (44)

4 (102)

³/₈ (10)

1³/₄
(44)   ³/₈
(10)

15¹/₂
(394)

5 (127)

¹/₈ (3)

1 (25)

2 (51)

1 (25)

1⁵/₈ (41) d

1¹/₄ (31) d

1⁵/₈ (41) d

1³/₈ (35) d

1¹/₂ (38) d

1⁵/₈ (41) d

1³/₈ (35) d

1⁵/₈ (41) d

1⁵/₈ (41) d

4 off

leg

③ Measure up and mark out the four legs for turning on the lathe as shown in the diagram. Be especially careful when turning in making the transition from square to round: do this with the point of a skew chisel, starting with repeated light cuts until the cut is continuous and to the required depth. Next turn the area in between, first to a cylinder and then to the chosen design.

④ Mark out the mortise-and-tenon joints. Traditionally these would have been plain bare-faced joints, leaving the rails and stretchers flush with the square surface of the legs. The joints on the long (or side) rails and stretchers are marked out and cut conventionally (see page 32), but those on the shorter (or end) rails and stretchers are angled and require special attention.

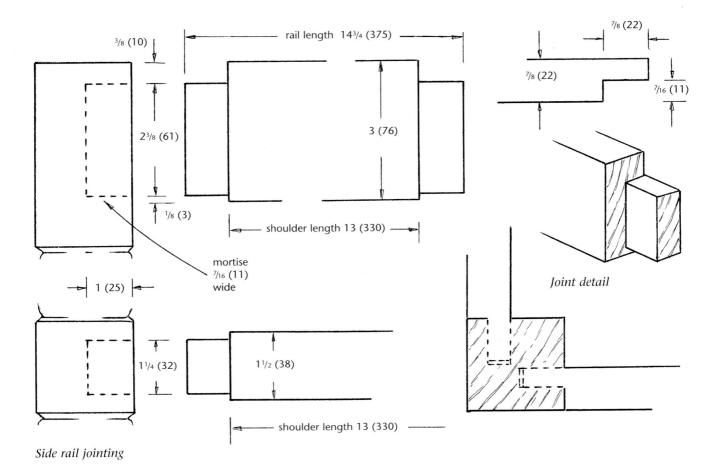

rail length 14³/₄ (375)

3/8 (10)

2³/8 (61)

3 (76)

1/8 (3)

shoulder length 13 (330)

mortise
7/16 (11)
wide

1 (25)

1¹/₄ (32)

1¹/₂ (38)

shoulder length 13 (330)

Side rail jointing

7/8 (22)

7/8 (22)

7/16 (11)

Joint detail

⑤ First mark out and cut the mortises to take the side rails and side stretchers as shown in the diagram, square to the face of the leg. Mark out and cut the bare-faced tenons to suit. Test fit individually into their respective mortises.

Detail of the joyned stool, showing the change in the leg from square to round and draw pegging of the joints

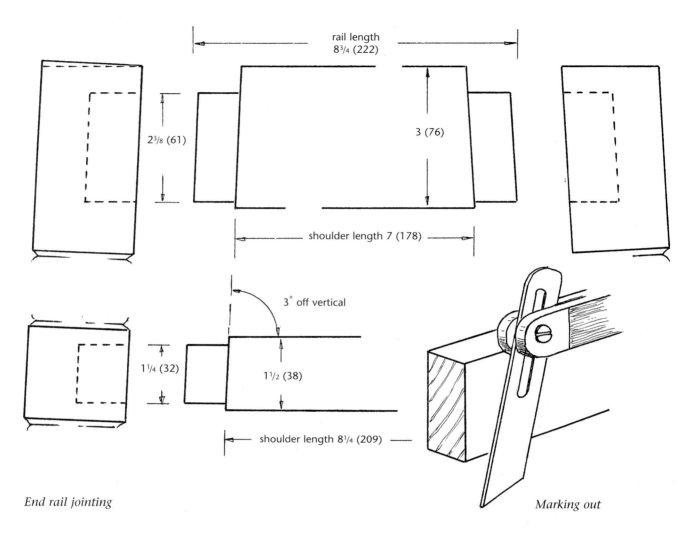

rail length
8¾ (222)

2⅜ (61)

3 (76)

shoulder length 7 (178)

3° off vertical

1¼ (32)

1½ (38)

shoulder length 8¼ (209)

End rail jointing

Marking out

⑥ Mark out the mortises for the end rails and stretchers as shown in the diagram. These are cut out at an angle of 3 degrees to the face of the legs, and guide lines marked on the surface will help when drilling and chiselling out the waste wood. Set a sliding bevel to 3 degrees to mark out these guide lines. Retain the same setting and mark out the corresponding bare-faced tenons. Mark the shoulders and the end of each tenon. Cut the tenons to the marked lines. Test fit individually into their respective mortises.

⑦ Have a trial dry assembly – without glue – and make any necessary adjustments. Trim the top ends of the canted legs to provide a level surface for the top when it is fitted.

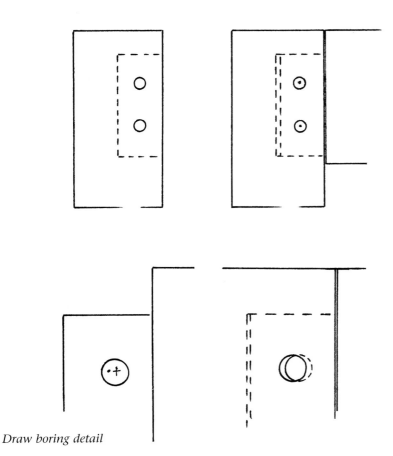

8 Prepare all the joints for pegging. (See below left and page 35 for the authentic draw bore method.) Make the required pegs.

9 With the stool components disassembled, work a bead along the lower edge of each top rail as a token decoration. A simple scratch stock may be made and used to achieve this (see the diagram below).

10 Clean all the components, removing unwanted marks, and prepare to glue up the complete frame. Begin by gluing up and fitting the two long side rails and stretchers: insert the joint-securing pegs, as described, and pull the joint shoulders up nice and tight. Wipe off any surplus glue. Cramps should not be required.

Draw boring detail

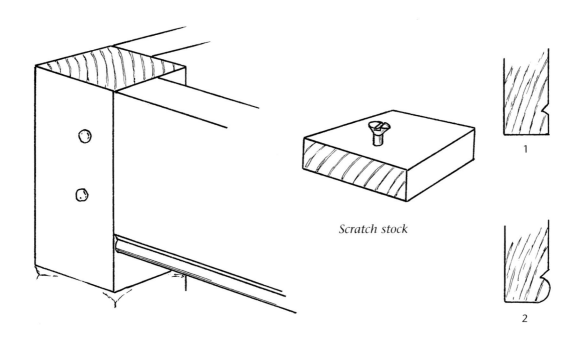

Scratch stock

1

2

11 Then glue up and add the end pieces, top rails and stretchers; insert the pegs, as before, and pull these joints up tight, ensuring that the canted shoulders meet the face of each leg correctly. Wipe off any surplus glue and leave to dry, standing on a level surface.

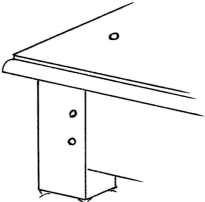

Fixing the top of the stool

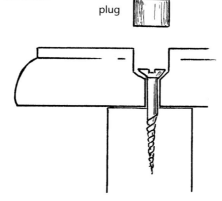

plug

12 While the frame is drying, complete the work on the seat piece. Clean up the glue joint and smooth as necessary. Cut the seat precisely to size and work a simple moulding of your choice all around its top edge as shown.

13 Traditionally seats were fixed to frames by pegs driven through holes bored through the seat and into the top rails and occasionally into the end grain on the legs. This is a perfectly adequate fixing if done correctly – that is, using square-headed pegs. And although it does not take account of any movement resulting from shrinkage, neither do the methods used in many modern reproductions of these stools. See the diagram for a suggested compromise.

14 Finally clean off all protruding pegs and clean the stool in preparation for finishing. Leave the pegs slightly proud for an authentic appearance.

15 To complete the authentic look of this stool the oak was lightly distressed and then stained and polished. Finishing details are given on page 39.

Trestle Table

··

The trestle table – perhaps the earliest

example of 'knock-down' portable

furniture – celebrates the durability of country

construction. It is from association with the use of

the wide top board of such tables that

the English language has gained expressions like

'board meeting' and 'board and lodging'.

Introduction The earliest of tables, the trestle type was originally a temporary affair, consisting of a single board placed, but not fixed, on two or more supports – the trestles. Arranged around the walls and the central fireplace of the typical Saxon hall, trestle tables were easily dismantled and taken away after each meal, which suited the communal living arrangements of the period. Furthermore, they were portable when the need arose to move on quickly, as it so often did in those troubled times.

The boards were at first quite narrow, intended only for a single row of sitters who sat with their backs to the wall – for safety, it is said, but also more convenient for food to be served from the other side and generally to enjoy the heat of the fire.

When life became more settled, household arrangements and, as a consequence, furniture changed too. The communal medieval hall gave way to separate rooms where fireplaces were set into the wall. Tables moved out into the middle of the room and became wider, and seating was provided on both sides. Rails were introduced to join pairs of trestles together, tenoned through and held with wedges. This resulted in a more stable table, but one which could still be dismantled for moving or storing.

Construction Details A ready means of disassembly is a major feature of the table described here. This is achieved by means of top joints with removable wooden pins or pegs which secure the top to the trestles and a wedged or loose key tenon on each end of the bottom stretcher rail which passes through each trestle. The top is made up from narrow boards, well seasoned and edge jointed, the joints strengthened by dowelling. Additional cross pieces are fitted across each end using a long, loose tongue. This method, known as end clamping, is used to prevent wide surfaces from twisting. A design which I have used successfully several times, this particular example was actually made by friend and working colleague Adrian Errey in his Sussex workshop.

Cutting List *(Add waste)*

No.	Item	in	mm
1	Top (to make)	$72 \times 34 \times 1^1/2$	$1829 \times 864 \times 38$
2	Trestles	$25 \times 14 \times 2$	$635 \times 356 \times 51$
2	Top bars	$26 \times 3 \times 2$	$660 \times 76 \times 51$
2	Bottom bars	$26 \times 3^1/2 \times 2$	$660 \times 89 \times 51$
4	Cross rails	$26 \times 3 \times 1^1/4$	$660 \times 76 \times 32$
1	Stretcher rail	$58 \times 4 \times 1^1/2$	$1473 \times 102 \times 38$
4	Round pegs	$8^1/2 \times 1 \times 1$	$216 \times 25 \times 25$
2	Wedges	$8 \times 2 \times 1/2$	$203 \times 51 \times 13$

Material Oak, ash, elm or pine.

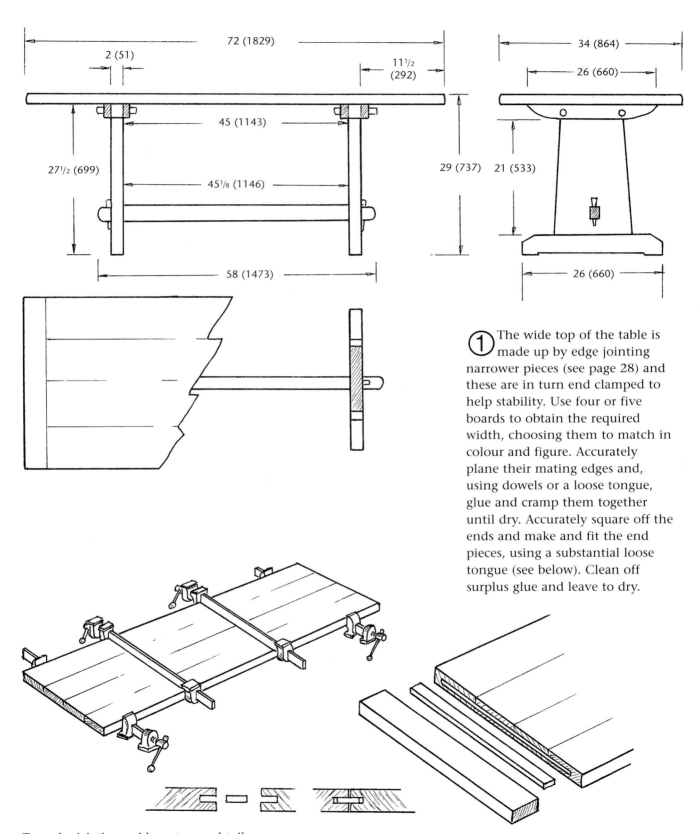

72 (1829)

2 (51)

11½ (292)

34 (864)

26 (660)

45 (1143)

27½ (699)

45⅛ (1146)

29 (737)

21 (533)

58 (1473)

26 (660)

① The wide top of the table is made up by edge jointing narrower pieces (see page 28) and these are in turn end clamped to help stability. Use four or five boards to obtain the required width, choosing them to match in colour and figure. Accurately plane their mating edges and, using dowels or a loose tongue, glue and cramp them together until dry. Accurately square off the ends and make and fit the end pieces, using a substantial loose tongue (see below). Clean off surplus glue and leave to dry.

Top: edge jointing and loose tongue detail

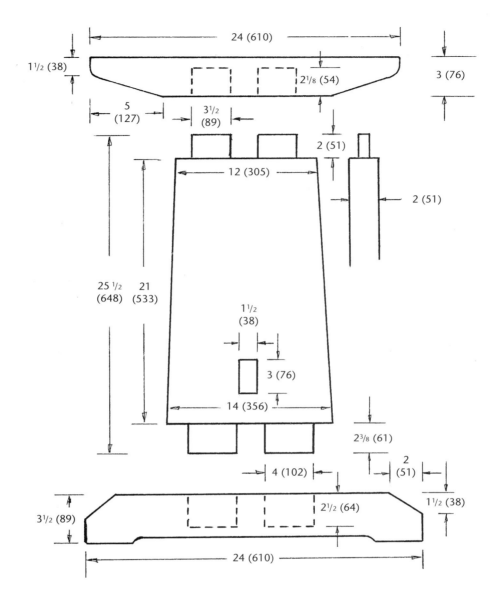

2 When all is dry and set, plane off any unevenness of the top surface, check that it is flat and put aside until later.

3 The two trestles are each made up from three pieces as shown. The dimensions supplied will give a table top height of 29 in (737 mm); the top is 1 1/2 in (38 mm) thick.

4 First cut the main trestles to size and shape; edge join narrow boards to make the required width if necessary. Cut the top and bottom bars to size and shape and mark out the position of the mortises which join the trestle pieces together. These are double mortise-and-tenon joints; single mortises cut into the bars would cause severe weakening of the joint areas.

5 Cut the mortises, keeping them accurately square and vertical. Mark out and cut the corresponding tenons on the main trestles. Try these joints for a good, neat fit; mark to identify and disassemble.

6 Mark out and cut the through mortises in each trestle to accommodate the centre rail.

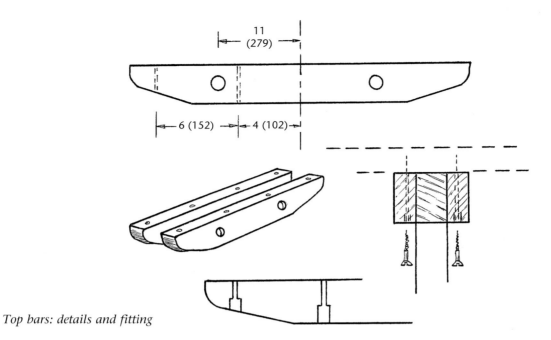

Top bars: details and fitting

7 The table top will be attached to the trestles by means of removable pegs passing through the trestle top bars which will be sandwiched between the pairs of close-fitting cross rails. In turn, these will be slot screwed to the underside of the table top. To obtain perfect alignment when drilling the holes for the securing pegs it is best to do so with the three parts of the 'sandwich' cramped firmly together.

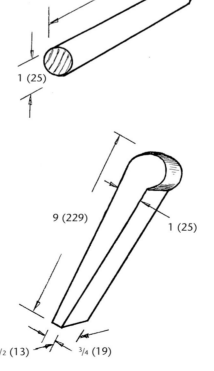

8 First cut out the required cross rails using a trestle top bar as a pattern. Clean up the rails and mark out and drill them for the slot screwing as shown in the diagram. Drill the large counter-bore first, according to the length of screw used. Then cramp the three pieces of each 'sandwich' together and mark out and drill the 1-in- (25-mm)-diameter peg holes, preferably using a saw-tooth Forstner bit, passing through all three pieces.

9 Make the four 1-inch (25-mm) pegs and test fit them in the drilled holes. They should be a tight fit but capable of removal with light blows from a mallet.

10 While the pieces are still cramped together, place them correctly on the underside of the table top and mark their position and the drilling points for the screws which will attach the two cross rails to the top. Clearly mark the mating pieces of the 'sandwich' to ensure that they go together in the same order later, then remove the cramps.

11 Glue up and assemble the two trestles and cramp until dry. After removing the cramps, chamfer the edges of the trestles using a spokeshave.

12 A partial assembly of the table can now be made. Carefully drill pilot holes in the underside of the table top at the marked positions for the cross rails. Screw the rails into place. Do not use glue. Test that the trestle top bars are a snug fit in between the cross rails, making any necessary adjustments. When satisfied, insert the securing pegs.

13 With the trestles in position measure the inside distance between them to confirm the shoulder length of the bottom rail. Keep this dimension generous – add a bare 1/8 in (3 mm) – so that the rail is a tight fit between the trestles; adding a little tension to the construction is preferable to having a loose fit. Knock out the securing pegs and remove the trestles.

14 Cut the bottom rail to length, cutting in the shoulders as shown below. Cut the mortises for the wedges; note how these intrude a little way into the mortises in the trestle to ensure that they pull up really tight when the wedges are fitted. Chamfer all four edges of the bottom rail.

15 Make the wedges as shown in the lower diagram opposite. They must be carefully made if they are to fit correctly and do their job properly in keeping the table stable. Decoratively shape the top part of the wedge as required.

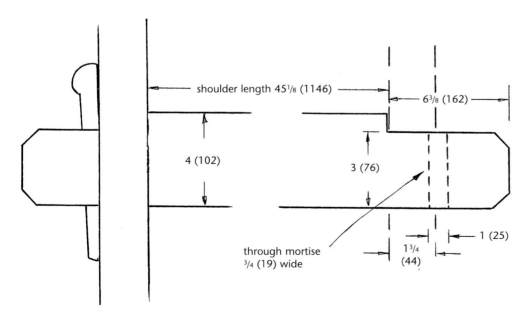

shoulder length 45 1/8 (1146)

6 3/8 (162)

4 (102)

3 (76)

1 (25)

through mortise
3/4 (19) wide

1 3/4 (44)

Bottom rail and tenon detail

16 The table can now be completely assembled in a standing position. Begin by putting the bottom rail in place in the two trestles and loosely knocking in the wedges. Then add the top to the trestles. Line up the drilled holes and tap in the round pegs to secure the top to the trestles. Tap the end wedges fully home and check for stability. When satisfied, disassemble for the final clean-up.

17 Scrape and clean all surfaces, paying particular attention to the upper surface of the top. Lightly chamfer all edges not previously chamfered. Reassemble the table, remembering to begin with the bottom rail. Tap the wedges and pegs in firmly.

18 A wax finish would be unsuitable for practical use. Instead, an oil finish is recommended. See page 39 for finishing details.

Details of the trestle table construction showing (above) the 'sandwich' of the trestle top bar and cross rails attached to the table top, with removable peg, and (left) the wedged or loose key tenon of the stretcher rail

Bookshelves

Books on a bookshelf reflect the owners'
nature – their past and present interests, their
dreams perhaps. The shelves need not be
too elaborate, but they must be sturdy:
the books themselves are decorative enough yet they
can be heavy, and shelves bowed beneath
their weight do not look good.

Introduction Shelf-and-cupboard combinations of this kind are loosely based upon the modern idea of the so-called 'Welsh' dresser. Such items of furniture have long been popular as they can be used to good purpose in different rooms in the home to store and display all manner of things, from dining room crockery to a collection of books. This particular piece was commissioned to occupy an alcove in a bedroom and the lower cupboard part is at a low height so that it might serve as a bedside table as well as fulfilling its use for storage and display purposes. If made for use elsewhere, this lower part could be built higher.

Construction Details The traditional jointing methods used in the main carcass of this piece of furniture result in a sturdy, rigid construction. The two lower, horizontal 'shelves' which form the bottom and top of the lower part are held in the side uprights in long dovetailed housings, while the top of the upper part is secured by substantial through dovetails. (Where the sides of the bookshelf are to be seen, lapped dovetails could be substituted here.) This dovetail construction adequately resists any sideways movement, allowing the intermediate shelves to remain free from the construction in order to facilitate their variable spacing. These loose shelves are supported on simple pegs located in pairs of holes drilled into the side uprights. The piece was made as a joint effort between myself and Adrian Errey using the facilities of his larger workshops.

Cutting List *(Add waste)*

No.	Item	in	mm
	MAIN CARCASS		
2	Side uprights	$70 \times 18 \times {}^{7}/_{8}$	$1778 \times 457 \times 22$
1	Lower part top	$31 \times 17^{1}/_{2} \times {}^{7}/_{8}$	$787 \times 445 \times 22$
1	Lower part bottom	$31 \times 18 \times {}^{7}/_{8}$	$787 \times 457 \times 2$
1	Top piece	$32 \times 11^{3}/_{4} \times {}^{7}/_{8}$	$813 \times 298 \times 22$
1	Cornice	$55 \times 3 \times {}^{7}/_{8}$	$1379 \times 76 \times 22$
1	Plinth	$31 \times 4 \times {}^{7}/_{8}$	$787 \times 102 \times 22$
1	Back (to make)	$66 \times 32 \times {}^{3}/_{8}$	$1676 \times 813 \times 10$
	LOOSE SHELVES		
3	Top part shelves	$30^{1}/_{4} \times 11 \times {}^{7}/_{8}$	$768 \times 279 \times 22$
1	Lower part shelf	$30^{1}/_{4} \times 16^{1}/_{2} \times {}^{7}/_{8}$	$768 \times 419 \times 22$
	CUPBOARD DOORS		
4	Stiles	$18^{1}/_{4} \times 2 \times {}^{7}/_{8}$	$464 \times 51 \times 22$
4	Rails	$13^{1}/_{2} \times 2 \times {}^{7}/_{8}$	$343 \times 51 \times 22$
2	Panels	$14^{3}/_{4} \times 11^{3}/_{4} \times {}^{1}/_{2}$	$375 \times 298 \times 13$

Material Pine, ash, cherry or beech.

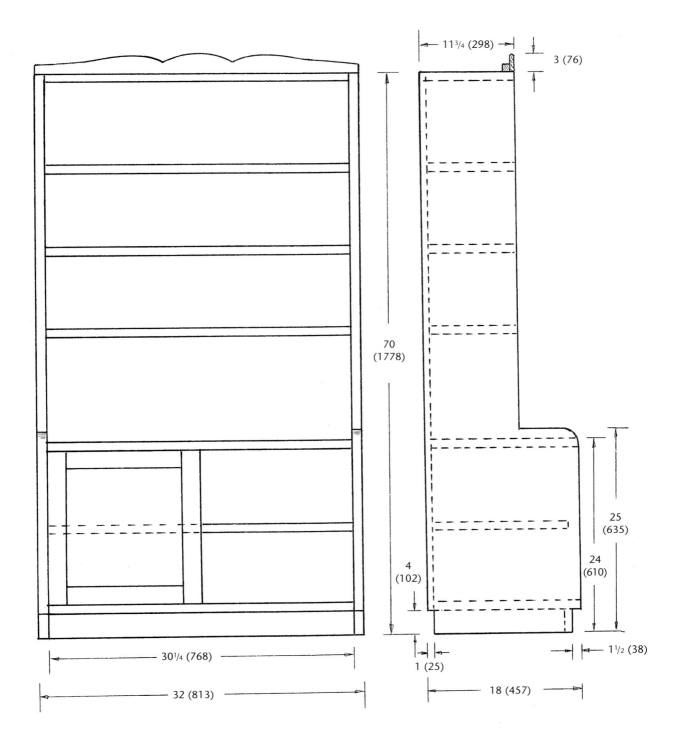

11¾ (298)

3 (76)

70
(1778)

30¼ (768)

32 (813)

4
(102)

1 (25)

25
(635)

24
(610)

1½ (38)

18 (457)

①Almost all the material for this project requires edge jointing in order to make up the wide boards required. Begin by making up the two side uprights using selected timber (see page 28 for information on edge jointing). If these are done first, further work on them can proceed while other edge joined boards, such as the various shelves and door panels, are glued and drying.

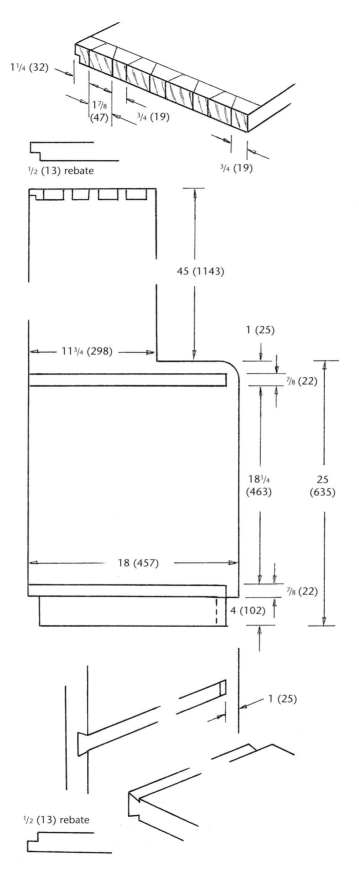

1¼ (32)

1⅞ (47)

¾ (19)

½ (13) rebate

¾ (19)

45 (1143)

11¾ (298)

1 (25)

⅞ (22)

18¼ (463)

25 (635)

18 (457)

⅞ (22)

4 (102)

1 (25)

½ (13) rebate

② Cut the two side uprights to their finished shape and size, round over and smooth the end grain of the lower part's top edges. Mark out for the dovetail housings which will accommodate the lower part's fixed top and bottom pieces. To ensure conformity these are best marked out with the uprights back-to-back, if workshop space permits.

③ The housings can be cut by hand, but they are more easily done with the aid of a router fitted with a dovetail cutter. Note that they are stopped housings, finishing short of the front edge by approximately 1 in (25 mm). The top and bottom pieces are notched back by this same amount at their front edge. Note that all the intermediate (loose) shelves and the top piece of the lower part are narrower by ½ in (13 mm) to allow for the back when fitted.

④ With the two wide top and bottom 'shelves' cut square and to the correct width and length, mark out and cut the mating dovetail on the end of each. Again the router may be used to good effect or they may be cut by hand. Remove the first 1 in (25 mm) or so of the dovetail to suit the stopped housing and test fit the joints. They should slide easily into position; if they are too tight, do not risk breaking the tail but ease it by careful chiselling or sanding. A smooth chamfer on the leading edge aids entry. When you are satisfied with them, put these items aside until later.

⑤ Next, cut the top piece accurately square to length and width and mark out the through dovetail joints as shown in the diagram on page 134.

⑥ Cut the dovetail joints (see page 38). Careful sawing should produce a fairly close fit first time, especially if you are working in soft wood. Trim as necessary to a neat, tight fit. Disassemble when satisfied.

⑦ The two side uprights, the wide, fixed bottom 'shelf' of the lower part and the top piece of the upper part all require rebating on their inside back edges to accommodate the back. This rebate is 1/2 in (13 mm) wide and 1/2 in (13 mm) deep. It can be cut by hand or with a router.

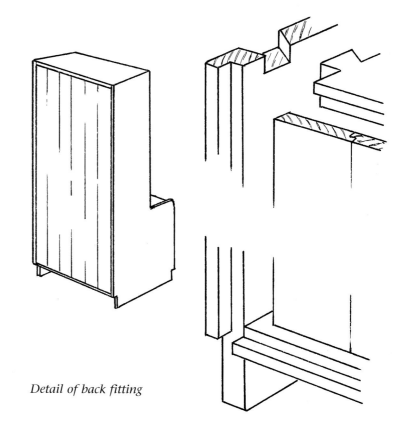

Detail of back fitting

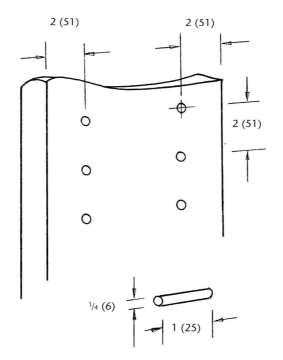

Detail of shelf pegs

⑧ The intermediate (loose) shelves are supported on pegs located in pairs of holes in the side uprights. These allow for alternative spacing of the shelves. The holes are drilled at 2-in (51-mm) centres. Wood or metal pegs may be used; they should be an easy matching fit in the drilled holes. Drill the holes carefully so as not to tear the wood grain.

⑨ Make the shelf pegs from wood dowel or metal rod, about 1/4 in (6 mm) diameter and about 1 in (25 mm) long. Remove any burr from sawing and round over the ends for easy insertion.

10 This is a good time to make the cut-away for the front plinth and the skirting clearance at the back. The measurements given for the latter may be altered to suit your own skirting height if necessary.

11 Now have a dry assembly (without glue) of the main carcass components, working on a level surface. First insert the bottom and middle 'shelves' into their respective dovetail housings in the side uprights and ensure that they all line up neatly at their front edges. Push the front plinth into position from below. Finally add the top, manipulating the dovetails into place and tapping down with a hammer while protecting the joint area with a piece of waste wood.

12 If all the 'shelves' were accurately cut square and to length, this dry assembly should proceed without problems. It should also hold together without cramping, although cramps can be used if necessary. Check for squareness, paying particular attention to the lower cupboard door opening.

13 When, satisfied, disassemble, clean off all unwanted marks and ensure that the surfaces are sanded smooth. Then apply glue where required and repeat the procedure described in stage 11. Check for squareness again and leave to dry.

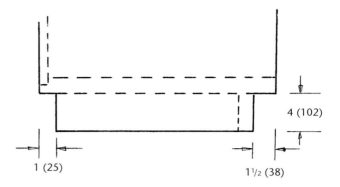

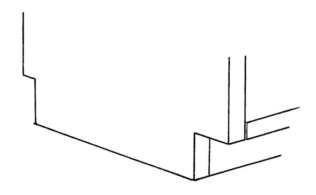

Front plinth and skirting clearance

14 After assembly, check the required length of the intermediate (loose) shelves and measure up for the cupboard doors. Although dimensions for these are given, it is best to take measurements from the respective openings in case there is a difference.

15 Cut the three intermediate shelves and the wider cupboard shelf to size and try them out on their peg supports. Ease the fit if necessary.

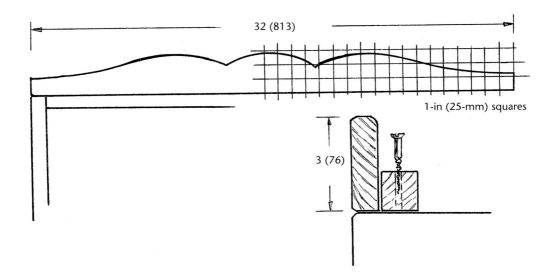

32 (813)

1-in (25-mm) squares

3 (76)

⑯ Complete the carcass by shaping and fitting the top cornice. Its top edge has a decorative bead, applied before fitting by use of a simple scratch stock (see page 121). The cornice is fixed on by means of screw blocks.

17 The two doors can now be made. The frames are 2 in (51 mm) wide and 7/8 in (22 mm) thick. The frames have haunched mortises and tenons and are grooved to accept the fielded door panels.

18 Cut the door frame components to length; be generous to make slightly oversize doors which can be trimmed to fit. Now make the grooves which accommodate the door panels, 3/8 in (10 mm) wide and 3/8 in (10 mm) deep. Cut the joint mortises, which are the same width as the groove and 1 3/8 inch (35 mm) deep.

19 Now cut the haunched tenons on the ends of the door rails and test fit in the mortises until satisfied. (See pages 33 and 34 for details of how to make this type of joint.)

Details of the bookshelves, showing (this page) one of the doors of the lower section and (opposite) a front top corner of the upper section – note the through dovetail joint and cornice moulding of the latter

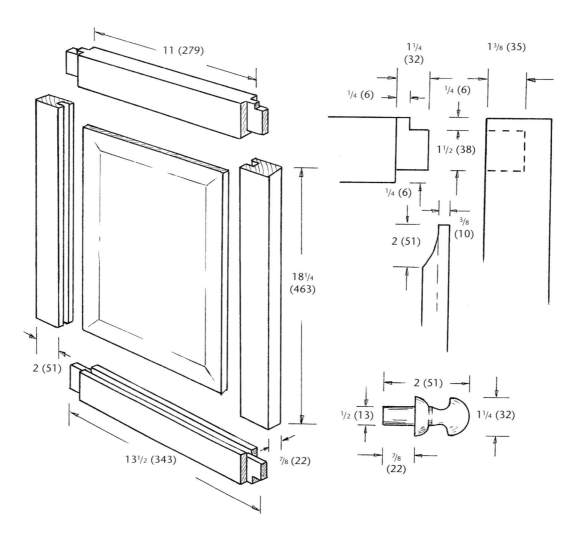

11 (279)

1¼ (32)

1³⁄₈ (35)

¼ (6)

¼ (6)

1½ (38)

¼ (6)

2 (51)

³⁄₈ (10)

18¼ (463)

2 (51)

2 (51)

13½ (343)

⁷⁄₈ (22)

½ (13)

1¼ (32)

⁷⁄₈ (22)

20 Check the measurements for the door panels and cut these to size. They should be slightly undersize to allow for movement. Then reduce the thickness at the edges – this is known as fielding – to fit into the groove already made in the door frames. This can be done by hand planing or by using a power router.

21 Have a dry assembly of the two doors and, when satisfied, glue the joints and reassemble. The panels are not glued in but left free to allow for movement. Check that the doors are square and not twisted, then allow to dry.

22 When the doors are dry, clean them up and try them in the cupboard opening, trimming them to a neat fit. Hang each of them on a pair of good butt hinges. Finish off by fitting a concealed catch and a pair of suitable turned wooden knobs.

23 Check that all pencil lines and dirty marks have been removed and apply a finish of your choice. This example was given a clear finish to enhance the grain of the pine, but it would look equally good painted. See page 39 for finishing advice.

Blanket Chest

When chests were more commonplace, clothing

was folded rather than hung.

Wardrobes changed all that, yet these simple

boxes are still popular today and add a

certain old-world charm to any room,

particularly when placed at the

foot of a bed.

Introduction Regarded by many as one of the earliest forms of furniture, the medieval oak chest, to which this is a kind of country cousin, once fulfilled an important multi-purpose role in the lives of our predecessors. Used primarily for storage, it also served as seat, table and sometimes bed in their sparsely furnished homes. Furthermore it was an important and necessary item for travel; in earlier times it was often kept ready for use at short notice during periods of social and political unrest. At sea it contained a sailor's entire belongings. The earliest chests were simply hollowed-out tree trunks, and we still refer to a large piece of travel luggage as a 'trunk'. Later, boarded chests nailed or pegged together and bound with iron straps became common, until the introduction of frame-and-panel construction brought about further developments in all forms of furniture making. In country areas, however, the boarded chest or box in an improved form continued in use, probably because it was easier to make and not too demanding on materials.

Construction Details Based on boarded chests common in rural areas on both sides of the Atlantic and throughout Europe, the chest described here is sturdily built in inexpensive pine. It incorporates substantial 'carpenter's' dovetails which form strong, interlocking corner joints. Well made, these joints also serve a decorative function. Constructed from single wide boards, the chest can be made using narrower boards edge joined together to give the required width. A broad plinth decorates the lower edge and optional rope handles add a nautical touch if required.

Cutting List (Add waste)			
No.	Item	in	mm
2	Sides	$36 \times 17^{1/2} \times {}^{7/8}$	$914 \times 445 \times 22$
2	Ends	$18 \times 17^{1/2} \times {}^{7/8}$	$457 \times 445 \times 22$
1	Bottom	$34 \times 16 \times {}^{7/8}$	$864 \times 406 \times 22$
1	Top or lid	$38 \times 19 \times {}^{7/8}$	$965 \times 483 \times 22$
2	Front mouldings	$38 \times 2 \times {}^{7/8}$	$965 \times 51 \times 22$
2	Back mouldings	$38 \times 2 \times {}^{7/8}$	$965 \times 51 \times 22$
2	End mouldings	$20 \times 2 \times {}^{7/8}$	$508 \times 51 \times 22$
1	Front inside batten	$36 \times 1^{1/2} \times {}^{7/8}$	$914 \times 38 \times 22$
1	Back inside batten	$36 \times 1^{1/2} \times {}^{7/8}$	$914 \times 38 \times 22$
2	End inside battens	$16 \times 1^{1/2} \times {}^{7/8}$	$406 \times 38 \times 22$
1	Top back batten	$36 \times 1^{1/2} \times {}^{7/8}$	$914 \times 38 \times 22$
1	Lid front batten	$38 \times 2 \times {}^{7/8}$	$965 \times 51 \times 22$
2	Lid end battens	$18 \times 2 \times {}^{7/8}$	$457 \times 51 \times 22$

Material Pine.

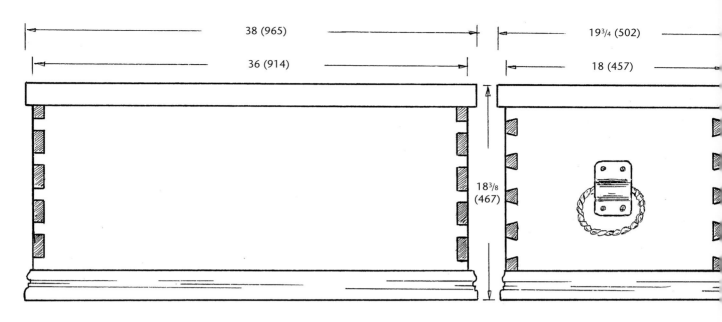

38 (965)   19³/4 (502)

36 (914)   18 (457)

18³/8 (467)

① The chest described here was made from wide boards of pine rescued from a redundant church just ahead of the demolition gang. When wide boards are unobtainable, it will be necessary to edge join narrower pieces to make up the required widths (see page 28).

② Choose the pieces with the best grain figure for the front and top. Then begin by cutting the front and back pieces and two end pieces to the correct length and width. Ensure that all their ends are square and sound.

③ Now mark out and cut the dovetail joints (see page 38). Follow the procedure of making the 'tails' first by carefully marking these out on each end of both of the end pieces. Follow the diagram, using the measurements given to space the tails. Note that the top and bottom tails are the largest at 2 in (51 mm), while the remaining ones are all of equal size at 1¹/2 in (38 mm).

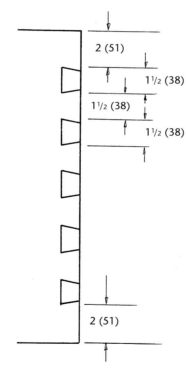

2 (51)

1¹/2 (38)

1¹/2 (38)

1¹/2 (38)

2 (51)

④ Saw out the marked tails. Cut carefully down to the depth line and remove the waste either now or later using a coping saw and sharp chisel.

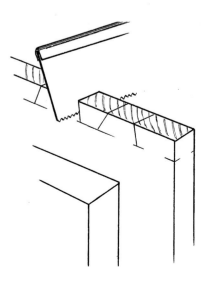

Then, using the cut tails as a template, mark out the 'pins' or sockets of the joints. Saw these out, taking care to cut on the waste side to ensure tight-fitting joints. Remove the waste by careful chiselling.

Test fit, without glue, the mating parts of the dovetail joints and make any necessary adjustments by careful paring with a sharp chisel. Too many test fits will result in gaps in the joint.

When you are satisfied, clean off any unwanted marks and prepare for assembly. Do this on a level surface. Put glue on the joint areas, press the sides and ends together and apply the necessary cramping pressure. Check that the work is square – do this by measuring across the diagonals. Remove any surplus glue and leave to dry.

Now fit the battens which support the bottom of the chest. First cut these to length, then fit them to the inside of the chest flush with its lower edge. The battens should be glued and may be either screwed or nailed into position.

Measure the inside of the chest and mark out the bottom panel slightly smaller than this. Cut the panel to size and fit it inside the chest. It can be fixed in place or left loose.

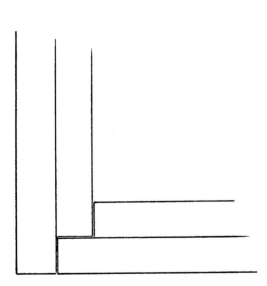

Detail of bottom battens and bottom fixing

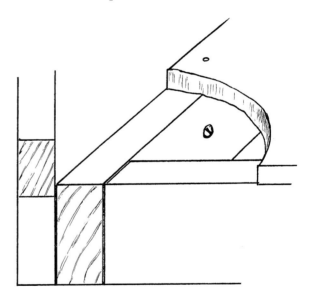

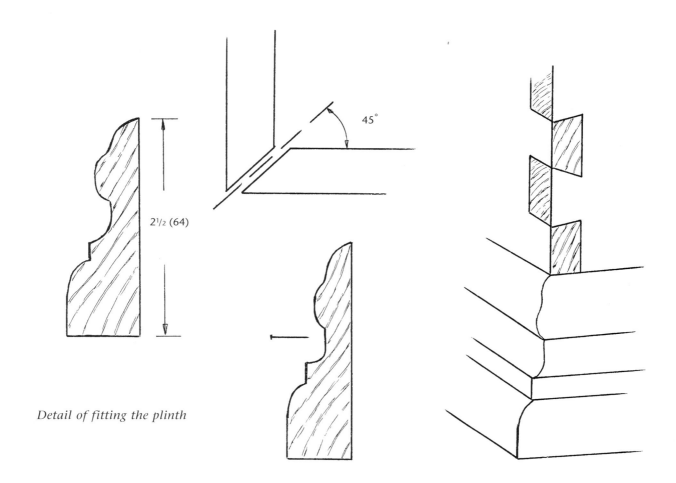

Detail of fitting the plinth

2½ (64)

45°

10 Fit the plinth moulding all around the outside bottom edge. This moulding can be bought in ready for use or made by hand or with a router and suitable cutter. Measure and cut the corner mitres with care to give neat, gap-free joints. Glue and panel pin the moulding into place and allow to dry.

11 Cut to length and fit the top back batten. This gives additional support to the top hinges. Glue and screw this into place flush with the top back edge as shown.

12 Now cut the top, or lid, to size. It should be slightly larger than the overall length and width, including the top back batten, of the chest so that it is not prevented from closing when the front and end battens are fitted. Carefully measure the dimensions of your chest to obtain the correct measurements – those given are for guidance only.

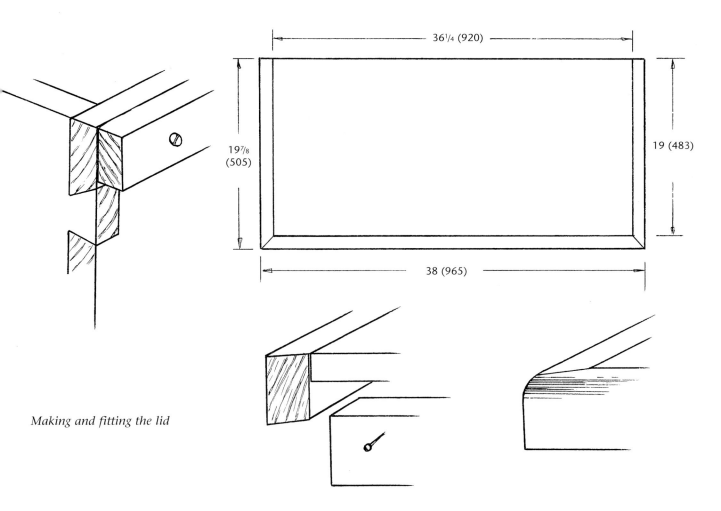

36¼ (920)

19⅞ (505)

19 (483)

38 (965)

Making and fitting the lid

13 Fit the front and end battens to the edge of the lid. Measure with care and cut the mitred corners to fit. Glue and screw into place. Conceal the fixing holes.

14 Try the lid for fit. Chamfer or round over the top edge all around to leave a smooth finish.

Detail of a corner of the blanket chest, showing the dovetail joint, rope handle fixing and moulded plinth

15 Mark out the position of the hinges as shown. Cut the required recesses for the hinges in the underside of the lid and into the back top edge of the chest. Then fit the hinges, first to the lid, then to the chest. Align correctly for a smooth opening and closing movement.

16 For safety's sake, fit a suitable stay or a cord to restrict the backward swing of the lid.

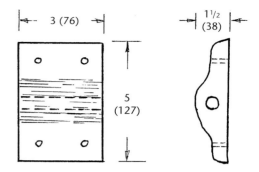

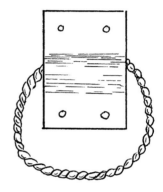

Detail of rope handle fixing

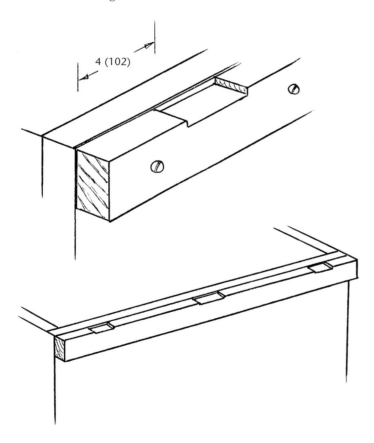

Hinging detail

17 Fit suitable substantial handles, either ready-made in iron or brass or home-made. Those used here were shaped as shown and screwed to the side of the chest. The rope is threaded through and spliced.

18 Several finishes would be equally suitable for this project. It could be painted and would lend itself to being 'distressed', or it could be stained and suitably 'aged', or it might be finished clear with varnish or oil. This example is finished with oil and wax. See page 39 for details.

Long Bench

Familiar wherever communal seating is
required, long benches such as the one
described here provide a useful alternative to separate
stools and chairs. Practical both indoors and
outside, benches make sensible and inexpensive
seating very much in keeping with
the country look.

Introduction While chairs were still the prerogative of those with status (see page 116), one of the most usual forms of seating for the common people was the bench. Multiple-seated benches satisfied the communal way of life in many a medieval hall and examples built to hold up to a dozen diners are not unkown. A stool is, by definition, a movable seat for one person, but if it is extended to accommodate more than one it becomes either a form or a bench. It is from the use of the lightweight, extended stool – the form – in many early schools, where pupils sat in strict order of their educational progress on the first, second or third row of forms, that school classes or grades continue to be referred to as 'forms'. Benches, on the other hand, are generally more sturdily constructed and some of the earliest were fixed, 'built-in' objects. In the British House of Commons members of parliament sit upon long, fixed benches; lesser members, who sit at the back, are known as backbenchers.

Benches were made in various styles, from the elaborate, turned and carved refectory type to those of trestle-like construction consisting of a single wide board top or seat mounted on a pair of trestle ends. The one described here is of the latter type, made as a companion to the trestle table described on page 123.

Construction Details The solid oak top or seat is made by edge jointing two or three narrower pieces together. Cross pieces mortised and tenoned across at each end ensure long-lasting stability and freedom from twisting. The sturdy trestles are double mortised and tenoned through the seat where they are wedged for further security. A central stretcher rail passes through each trestle and is secured by means of a traditional wedged or loose key tenon. The bench described is made to suit a trestle table over 6 ft (approximately 2 m) long, but it can easily be reduced in overall length if a smaller version is required.

Cutting List (Add waste)		
No. Item	in	mm
3 Long top pieces	$76 \times 4^{1}/4 \times 1^{1}/2$	$1930 \times 108 \times 38$
2 Top end pieces	$12^{3}/4 \times 4 \times 1^{1}/2$	$324 \times 102 \times 38$
2 Main trestles	$16^{3}/4 \times 7 \times 1^{3}/4$	$425 \times 178 \times 44$
2 Bottom bars	$12^{3}/4 \times 3 \times 1^{3}/4$	$324 \times 76 \times 44$
1 Stretcher	$60 \times 2^{1}/2 \times 1^{1}/2$	$1524 \times 64 \times 38$

Material Oak.

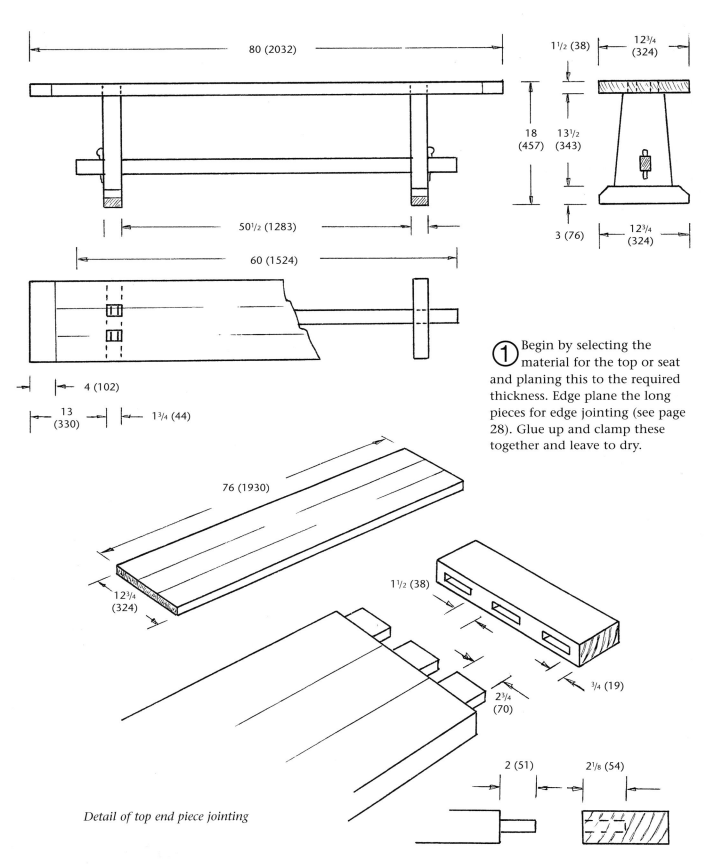

80 (2032)

1½ (38)

12¾ (324)

18 (457)

13½ (343)

3 (76)

12¾ (324)

50½ (1283)

60 (1524)

4 (102)

13 (330)

1¾ (44)

① Begin by selecting the material for the top or seat and planing this to the required thickness. Edge plane the long pieces for edge jointing (see page 28). Glue up and clamp these together and leave to dry.

76 (1930)

12¾ (324)

1½ (38)

¾ (19)

2¾ (70)

2 (51)

2⅛ (54)

Detail of top end piece jointing

2 Mark out and cut the mortises in the end pieces. Ensure that these are kept accurate and square; note that they are cut slightly deeper than the prescribed tenon length.

3 When the long top pieces are dry, square off both ends and mark out and cut the end tenons. Test fit the end pieces and, when they are satisfactory, glue up and leave to dry.

4 Now prepare the material for and make up the two trestles as shown. Cut the main part to size and shape, cut the ends square and mark out the top and bottom tenons. Note that the top tenons will go through the full thickness of the seat, while the bottom ones are 'blind', are shouldered and have a central haunch. Then cut the bottom bars to size and shape and mark out the double mortises in their top edge.

5 Cut the double mortises in the bottom bars. Cut the corresponding tenons already marked out on the main trestle pieces and test fit until satisfied.

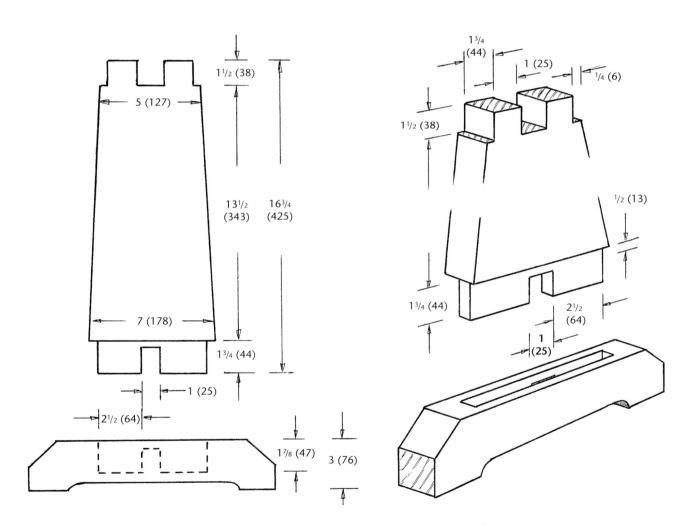

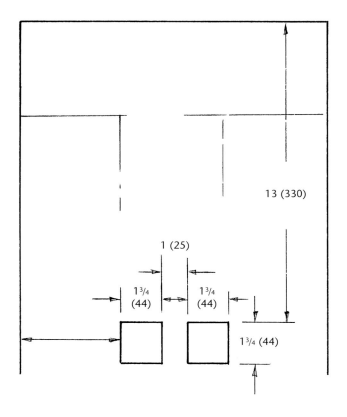

13 (330)

1 (25)

1³/₄ (44)   1³/₄ (44)

1³/₄ (44)

⑥ Next mark out the position of the top mortises through the seat and cut these accurately to size. Take care not to round over or crush the top edge to ensure a neat-fitting joint. Cut the corresponding tenons already marked out on the main trestle pieces and test fit until satisfied. The tenons should just protrude through the seat and be cleaned off flush later after being wedged to tighten the joint for extra security (see stage 13).

⑦ Now is a good time to have a dry assembly – without glue – to check progess. Do this on a level surface. Fit the bottom bars to the trestles and place the top (seat) on to the trestles. Check that everything goes together correctly so far.

⑧ With the trestles in position, measure the exact distance between the two to ascertain the required shoulder length of the stretcher rail. Keep this measurement generous to ensure that the stretcher is a tight fit between the trestles. (The dimension given is only a guide.) Disassemble, glue the bottom bars on to their respective trestles and leave to dry.

Detail of the long bench, showing the end of the stretcher rail and the loose key tenon with decorative wedge

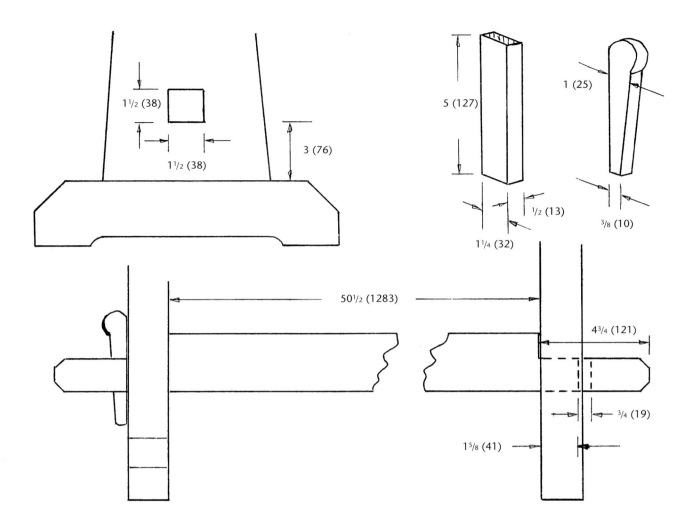

1½ (38)

1½ (38)

3 (76)

5 (127)

1 (25)

½ (13)

³/₈ (10)

1¼ (32)

50½ (1283)

4³/₄ (121)

³/₄ (19)

1⁵/₈ (41)

⑨ Mark out the position of the through mortises for the stretcher tenon on each of the made-up trestles as shown. cut both mortises carefully.

⑩ Plane the stretcher to thickness and cut to length, then mark out and cut in the shoulders as shown. Mark out and cut the mortises for the loose wedges; note that these intrude a little way into the mortise so that the wedges pull up tight.

⑪ Make the two wedges as shown. Test fit individually to obtain a good, tight fit.

12 The bench can now be assembled – again without further gluing – for a final check. Begin by putting the stretcher in position in the two trestles; fit the stretcher wedges. Then add the top (seat) to this assembly. The bench can be put together only by following this sequence.

13 With the bench assembled, mark the position of the wedges which will tighten the top tenons in the seat. These must go in at right angles to – that is, across – the grain of the seat: the wedges could split the seat if knocked in along its grain. When this is done, disassemble for the final details and clean-up.

14 Saw down each top tenon for the wedges as shown. Make the required number of wedges. Lightly chamfer or 'soften' by rounding over all the exposed edges of the bench. Clean off all unwanted surface marks and prepare for the final assembly.

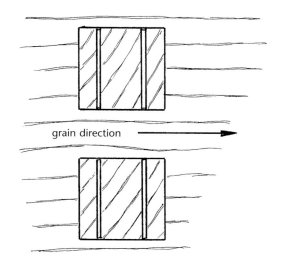

grain direction ⟶

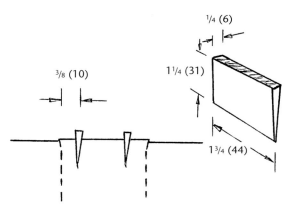

Detail of tenon wedging

15 Assemble the bench, beginning by putting the stretcher into the trestles and inserting the two loose wedges. Do not use glue for this. Then put glue in the mortise joints in the seat and bring the seat down on to the trestle tenons. Level up, tap the tenon wedges into place, wipe off the surplus glue and leave to dry and set.

16 Trim off the protruding tenon wedges and level off the tenon ends as required.

17 As for the trestle table, an oil finish is recommended for this type of bench. The bench shown in the photographs was stained before oil was applied. See page 39 for finishing information.

Sources and Courses

Wood

UK
John Boddy
Riverside Sawmills
Boroughbridge
N. Yorks
YO5 9LU

Craft Supplies
Millers Dale
Buxton
Derbys
SK17 8SN

South London Hardwoods
12 Belgrave Road
London
EC25 5AN

West and Sons Ltd
Selham
Petworth
W. Sussex
GU28 OPU

USA
Colonial Hardwoods
Camron Brown
Springfield
VA 22153

Peter Lang Company
3115 Porter Creek Road
Santa Rosa
CA 95404

Talarico Hardwoods
Route 3 Box 3268
Mohnton
PA 19540-9339

Willard Brothers
300 Basin Road
Trenton
NJ 08619

Hardware

UK
H. E. Saville
9 St Martins Place
Scarborough
N. Yorks
YO11 2QH

Woodfit Ltd
Chorley
Lancs
PR6 7EA

USA
Paxton Hardware Ltd
PO Box 256
Upper Falls
MD 21156

Whitechapel Ltd
PO Box 136
Wilson
WY 83014

Abrasives

UK
CSM Trade Supplies
95–96 Lewes Road
Brighton
BN2 3QA

USA
Econ Abrasives
PO Box 1628
Frisco
TX 75034

Finishing Materials

UK
Liberon
Learoyd Road
New Romney
Kent
TN28 8XV

Morrell Co. Ltd
Woodley
Stockport
Cheshire
SK6 1RN

Rustin Ltd
Waterloo Road
Cricklewood
London
NW2 7TX

USA
Hut Products
15361 Hopper Road
Sturgeon
MO 65284

Liberon Supplies
PO Box 86
Mendocino
CA 95460

Velvit Products
PO Box 1741
Appleton
WI 54911

Seating Materials

UK
Jacobs Young & Westbury
Bridge Road
Haywards Heath
W. Sussex
RH16 1UA

USA
H. H. Perkins & Co.
10 South Bradley Road
Woodbridge
CT 06525

Tools (Mail Order)

UK

Axminster Tools
Chard Street
Axminster
Devon
EX13 5DZ

Craft Supplies
Millers Dale
Buxton
Derbys
SK17 8SN

Fine Wood & Tool Store
Boroughbridge
N. Yorks
YO5 9LJ

USA

Constantine
2050 Eastchester Road
Bronx
New York
NY 10461

Garratt Wade Co.
161 Sixth Avenue
New York
NY 10013

Lee Valley Tools Ltd
12 East River Street
Ogdensburg
NY 13669

Where to See Furniture

UK

Geffrye Museum
Kingsland Road
Shoreditch
London
E2 8EA

Temple Newsam House
Leeds
W. Yorks
LS15 OAE

Towneley Hall
Burnley
Lancs
BB11 3RQ

Victoria & Albert
  Museum
South Kensington
London
SW7 2RL

USA

Colonial Williamsburg
PO Box C
Williamsburg
VA 23817

Metropolitan Museum of Art
Fifth Avenue & 87th Street
New York
NY 10028

Smithsonian Institution
National Museum of
  American History
12th & Constitution Avenue
Washington DC 20560

Winterthur Museum
Winterthur
Delaware
DE 19735

Courses

UK

Buckinghamshire College
High Wycombe
Bucks
HP11 2JZ

Jack Hill Workshops
PO Box 20
Midhurst
W. Sussex
GU29 OJD

Rycotewood College
Thame
Oxford
OX9 2AF

West Dean College
Chichester
W. Sussex
PO18 OQZ

USA

Centre for Furniture
  Crafts
25 Mill Street
Rockport
ME 04856

College of the
  Redwoods
440 Alger Street
Fort Bragg
CA 95437

North Bennet Street
  School
39 North Bennet Street
Boston
MS 02113

Warwick Country
  Workshops
PO Box 665
Warwick
NY 10990

Bibliography

Bennett, Michael, *Discovering & Restoring Antique Furniture*, Cassell, 1990.

Bly, John, *Discovering English Furniture*, Shire Publications, 1981.

Gilbert, C., *English Vernacular Furniture 1750–1900*, Yale University Press,1991.

Hill, Jack, *Making Family Heirlooms*, David and Charles, 1985.

Hill, Jack, *Country Chair Making*, David and Charles, 1993.

Hill, Jack, *Country Woodworker*, Mitchell Beazley, 1995.

Joy, Edward, *Antique English Furniture*, Ward Lock, 1981.

Kettell, R. H., *Pine Furniture of Early New England*, Dover Publications, 1956.

Knell, David, *English Country Furniture*, Barrie and Jenkins, 1992.

Price, Bernard, *The Story of English Furniture*, BBC Publications, 1978.

Shea, John, *Antique Country Furniture of North America*, Reinhold, 1973.

Sparkes, Ivan, *English Domestic Furniture 1100–1837*, Spurbooks, 1980.

INDEX